A-Z OF NORTH WALES

Compiled by Dewi & Pamela Roberts

JOHN JONES

A - Z OF NORTH WALES

Compiled by Dewi and Pamela Roberts.

First published March 1997

Copyright reserved, text, title and design, the publishers.

The compilers and publishers believe the information contained herein to be accurate. They take no responsibility for any errors, or their consequences, that may inadvertently be included. If any errors or significant omissions are discovered by a reader, it would be appreciated if the publishers were informed. Any suggestions regarding new entries would also be gratefully received.

Cover design and illustrations by Chris Neale Graphics.

Printed in Wales by CIT Printing Services, Haverfordwest.

Distributed by The Welsh Books Council Distribution Centre, Llanbadarn, Aberystwyth.

Published by JOHN JONES PUBLISHING LTD., Barclays Bank Chambers, St. Peter's Square, Ruthin, Denbighshire.

ISBN 1 871083 95 8.

COMPILERS' INTRODUCTION

Despite the fact that the topography and history of North Wales have been the subject of many books, we felt that a publication of information in inexpensive, booklet format would be welcomed by visitors to the region as well as residents.

In the entries which follow, the reader will find concise information on towns, villages, lakes, rivers, mountains, historical events and literary references. We have selected the more interesting locations and features.

The southern border of North Wales has been drawn from the mouth of the River Dyfi, in the west, including Machynlleth, across eastwards to just south of Llanfyllin, joining the English border near Oswestry.

Because North Wales is an area of outstanding natural beauty, full of historical and cultural associations — where the past lives so strongly in the present — the compilation of this publication has been something of 'a labour of love'.

We hope it will lead you to new interesting places, and help you enjoy the area.

Dewi and Pamela Roberts

Denbigh

Autumn, 1996

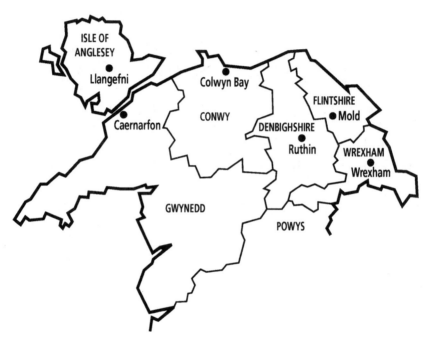

The new North Wales counties and their administration headquarters locations.

A

ABER, Gwynedd (Pop. 284)
(Aber — where two water meet)
2 miles SW of Llanfairfechan on A55. Woodland walk of 2 miles leads to spectacular waterfall (170ft). Reputed to be site of palace of Llewelyn the Great.

ABERAMFFRA, Gwynedd
Off Barmouth-Dolgellau A496 road. Entrance on sharp bend at bottom of Aberamffra hill. A lost harbour which was used for export of wool. Principal port on Cambrian coast in C17th, and shipbuilding also book place here. Popular for fishing.

ABERDARON, Gwynedd (Pop. 1,175)
Daron: goddess of oak trees. Village on tip of Llŷn Peninsula at end of B443. Bardsey pilgrims sheltered in church here while awaiting their sailings. Famous poet R. S. Thomas was rector of parish for many years.

ABERDESACH, Gwynedd
On Caernarfon-Pwellheli A499 road. Pebbly beach and much favoured by dinghy owners. Good parking facilities.

ABERDYFI, Gwynedd (Pop. 1,260)
16 miles S of Mawddach and W of Machynlleth on A493. Resort on Dyfi estuary, much favoured for fishing. Legend relates that a city lies under Cardigan Bay at this point which inspired song *The Bells of Aberdyfi*. Maritime museum.

ABERERCH, Gwynedd
Takes name from Erch river.
2 miles east of Pwllheli off A499. Village has sandy beach, ancient church, with striking bell tower.

ABERFFRAW, Anglesey
On A480 21 miles from Menai Bridge. Important historical site. Was main court of Princes of Gwynedd in Middle Ages. Archaelogical evidence of very early settlement. Branwen and Matholwch in *The Mabinogion* married here.

ABERGELE, Conwy
Gele — stream running through the town. (Pop. 14,500)
Former market town now by-passed by A55, a mile from coast. St. Michael's good example of double-naved church and occupies site of Celtic monastery. Poet Coleridge recorded his reaction to mixed bathing on beach in 1794.

ABERGLASLYN PASS, Gwynedd
Lying between the 498 and 4085 and rising to 2,566 ft. Walkers can commence ascent from point close to Beddgelert's Goat Hotel. Noted for scenic beauty.

ABERGYNOLWYN, Gwynedd
Village in Dysynni valley between Tywyn and Tal-y-Llyn. Terminus of small-gauge railway from Tywyn. A starting point for ascent of Cader Idris.

ABERSOCH, Gwynedd (Pop. 910)
Can be reached on A499. This Llŷn village popular with sailing boat enthusiasts. Very popular holiday site, with many caravans. Nearby St. Tudwal's Island has lighthouse, no longer in use.

ARDDU LAKE, Gwynedd (GR 6055) (Llyn Arddu)
Access on foot from footpath. Twin lake to Glaslyn. Behind is vertical precipice of Clogwyn dur Arddu. 5 acres at height of 1,901 ft.

AFONWEN, Flintshire
Village on River Wheeler on the A541 Mold-Denbigh road. Pwllgwyn Hotel is reputed to have once been the home of a prince. Hitching posts still preserved. Afonwen Craft Centre now occupies site where a woollen mill operated during the Industrial Revolution.

ALAW RIVER, Anglesey (Afon Alaw)
Flows through NW of island, and has source at Glasgraig. It flows into sea between Llanfachraeth and Llangyhaned. Near Llanddeusant is Bedd Branwen, which links river with story of the unfortunate Branwen in *The Mabinogion*. According to this source she is buried on the river bank.

AMLWCH, Anglesey (Around muddy water) (Pop. 3,700)
Town in N part of island. Evolved because of copper mining in area in C18th. Harbour constructed for export purposes. Today oil terminal where supertankers discharge supplies. Not primarily a resort town.

ANGLESEY (Ynys Môn)
Largest island off the Welsh coast, approached from mainland over Telford's Menai suspension bridge. A5 crosses island and extends over an embankment to Holy Island (see separate entry) and Holyhead. Island cover 290 square miles (175,811 acres) and measures 23 miles from SE to NW and 21 miles from NE to SW. Flat landscape; highest point 720ft. The county boundary re-organisation of 1995, made it a unitary County Borough. County offices: Isle of Anglesey Council, Llangefni, Anglesey, LL77 7TW. Tel (01248) 750032.

ARDUDWY
Coastal region situated between the Vale of Ffestiniog and the Mawddach Estuary through which the A496 runs. Communities include Maentwrog, Talsarnau, Harlech and Barmouth.

ARENIGS, Gwynedd

The 2 Arenigs tower over barren moorland area known as the Migneint (over 1,000 ft) between B4391 and A5.

ARTHOG, Gwynedd
On A493 between Dolgellau and Fairbourne. Village near S end of Mawddach Bridge facing the estuary. In picturesque setting between sea and Cader Idris.

ARTRO, Gwynedd
Stream in Artro valley in Rhinogs, surrounded by attractive woodland scenery. Interesting rock formations.

B

BACHEGRAIG WOODLAND TRAIL, Denbighshire
Take A541 Trefnant-Bodfari road and turn L at crossroads. Proceed for one mile until you see Bachegraig at the end of a drive on your R. 40 acres of broadleaved local woodland and a delightful walk. Small charge made. Pay at farmhouse. Bachegraig visited by Mrs. Thrale and Dr. Samuel Johnson on visit to Wales in 1774. Built in 1567 by Sir Richard Clough. It is one of the earliest examples in Wales of brick in domestic architecture.

BALA, Gwynedd (Bala; outlet) (Pop. 2,000)
Small town on A494 between Corwen and Dolgellau. Situated on edge of Llyn Tegid, largest natural lake in Wales. Town and general area very important in history of nonconformist religion and theological college situated here. Scenic lakeside railway and watersports. When John Byng visited the town in 1781 he discovered that in the depths of Winter ducks froze to the surface of the lake, providing a source of food for the local peasants. But he also tells us that "there were no skaters".

BALA LAKE, Gwynedd (Llyn Tegid) (GR9134)
Largest natural lake in Wales covering 1,123 acres. Charter granted in 1200 for fishing rights to monks at Basingwerk Abbey. Arthurian and Mabinogion associations. Legend relates tale of wicked Prince Tegid whose palace was on valley floor before lake came. He failed to heed a warning of the coming flood. "Teggie", a reported creature, is currently attracting some attention. Lakeside railway.

BANGOR, Gwynedd (Pop. 16,100)
Name probably derived form ban (bond) and cor (woven) a reference to protective hedge woven to protect church. University city on Menai Straits approached from north on A55, from south on A487. Bishopric since 546, this making it oldest in Britain. Cathedral founded by St. Deniol in C6th. University established 1883, now part of University of Wales. Theatr Gwynedd prestigious regional theatre. In 1897 *A. G. Bradley* visited the town and, while inspecting the Cathedral, reflected that "... to talk about what has been done on this time-honoured spot, would be to write a history of Wales."
BANGOR-ON-DEE, Wrexham (Bangor-is-y-Coed)

Take A545 from Wrexham for 5 miles. Village was site of ancient monastery, founded prior to 180AD. In C7th Saxons attacked it, murdered some of the monks and destroyed it. Surviving monks sought refuge on Bardsey Island. Fine C17th bridge, said to have been designed by Inigo Jones.

BANWY RIVER, Gwynedd (Afon Einion)
Leave Welshpool by A458 Llangadfan road. River source above Llangadfan and it runs close to the line of the Welshpool and Llanfair Light Railway.

BARDSEY ISLAND, Gwynedd (Yns Enlli)
3 miles off the mainland and Aberdaron. Important centre for religious pilgrimages in Middle ages; three visits to Bardsey were equivalent to one to Rome. Had its own king till 1926. Accommodation available for visitors. Brenda Chamberlain described her 15 year period here in book *Tide-race*.

BARMOUTH, Gwynedd (Pop. 3,000)
On A496 at mouth of Mawddach estuary. Situated between sea and steep hill behind town, it evolved as resort in Victorian period. Important in maritime history of region. The National Trust purchased first property here in 1895, 41/2 acres known as Dinas Oleu. Maw means broad while Mawddach means overflowing water.

BASINGWERK ABBEY, Flintshire
On A458 and 1/2 mile beyond Greenfield on road from Flint to Prestatyn. Circa 1131, this Cistercian site was founded by Ranulfe, second Earl of Chester. Original community probably attracted there by presence of nearby holy well. Dissolved in 1535. Visited by Gerald of Wales on his tour of Wales in 1188.

BEAUMARIS, Anglesey (Pop. 1,970)
Generally accepted derivation of name is from French beau, beautiful, and maree, sea-place by the beautiful sea. On A505 two miles beyond Menai Bridge. Popular yachting centre. Edwardian castle. Old gaol in Steeple Lane, now tourist attraction. Open June-September. Museum of Childhood, Castle St (Easter-Nov.). Annual arts festival. One of the most attractive seaside towns in North Wales.

BENLLECH, Anglesey
Family holiday resort on A5025 between Menai Bridge and Amlwch. Cliffs and extensive beach. Popular with bird-watchers and landscape artists. Many holiday cottages.

BERSHAM, Wrexham. S of Wrexham off A483. Early centre of the iron industry founded by John Wilkinson in C18th. Iron ceased to be manufactured here in 1820. Combination of coal, iron and waterpower near at hand made it ideal site for smelting and casting. A heritage and industrial archeological trail is now situated here. Well worth a visit.
BERWYN HILLS

Extensive moorland area through which the B4500 takes the motorist from Chirk to Lanrhaeadr-ym-Mochnant. Much Forestry Commission land in a region which has strong associations with Owain Glyndwr and his skirmishes with enemies.

BEDDGELERT, Gwynedd (Gelert's Grave) (Pop. 910)
Fame of village arose from legend of Llewelyn, Prince of Gwynedd and faithful hound Gelert. Grave of dog, two fields from village centre, was early attempt to dupe tourists in eighteenth century and was invention of local inn keeper. Good fishing.

BEDDGELERT FOREST, Gwynedd
1 mile N of Beddgelert. Good range of amenities. Waymarked walks, picnic sites and campsites.

BEDDGELERT MOUNTAIN ROAD, Gwynedd
From Beddgelert take A498 for 3 miles towards Capel Curig. Take the road after Llyn Dinas and turn R over Glaslyn river. 4 miles of spectacular scenery: rivers, valleys, waterfalls. Everything here lives up to Borrow's description of Wales as 'wild'.

BETHESDA, Gwynedd
Original name Cilfoden, but present name owes origin to congregational chapel of 1819. Could be regarded as stereotype of Welsh industrial village. Slate slag heaps are the legacy of its history. The Penrhyn family owned the quarries. The first major quarrying strike occurred here in 1900 (See Penrhyn Castle). On A5 between Capel Curig and Bangor.

BETWS GARMON, Gwynedd

Conwy Valley Railway, Betws-y-Coed

4 miles from Caernarfon on 4085. Good centre for pony trekking and walking in Snowdon foothills to Moel Eilio (2,382 ft) and Mynydd Mawr (2,290 ft.).

BETWS-Y-COED, Conwy (Pop. 790) (Birch Wood on Hilly Slopes)
Village in Conwy Valley on A5 between Corwen and Capel Curig. Swallow Falls (11/2 mile beyond village) much visited, as is Fairy Glen. Many shops and hotels catering for tourists. Popular with C19th artists. Miniature railway and railway museum a focal point for tourists. Run by the enterprising Colin Cartwright.

BLAENAU FFESTINIOG, Conwy. Blaen-heads of the valley
Town on A470 on A496 between Dolwyddelan and Llan Ffestiniog. History strongly associated with slate quarrying. But since decline of this industry tourism has replaced it. Llechwedd Slate Caverns recreate Victorian working conditions while nearby Gloddfa Ganol Museum will take you on tour on site of what was once world's biggest slate mine. The Llechwedd deep mine tour is an amazing experience, visiting caverns inside a mountain. Ffestiniog Power Station S of town.

BOCHLWYD LAKE (Llyn Bocklwyd), Gwynedd. GR 6559
On one of the Glyderau group, 1,805 ft. up rocky cliffs of Tryfan. Stream plunges 800 feet in 3/4 mile. Arthurian legend links Bedivere to this site.

BODDELWYDDAN, Denbighshire
Village off A55 between St. Asaph and Abergele. St. Margaret's Church ('The Marble Church') popular with tourists. 200 ft. spire. In cemetery are graves of Canadian soldiers who died during a mutiny in 1919 while they were awaiting a sailing to take them to their home country. Bodelwyddan Castle (C19) combines hotel, leisure complex, exhibition area, concert venue, cafe and shop. Surrounded by extensive grounds.

BODFARI, Denbighshire
Bod-dwelling place. Fari from Varis, Roman station in area. Village in Vale of Clwyd, 4 miles from Denbigh on A543 Mold road. In 19th century antiquarians found many relics of Roman occupation in area, inc. urns, fragments of weapons, etc. Church dedicated to St. Stephen.

BODLONDEB, Conwy
Sheer tree-covered mountain slopes above Conwy estuary, sheltering Conwy and facing Deganwy.

BODNANT GARDENS, Conwy
8 miles S of Llandudno. National Trust property, laid out in 1875. Cedars, stately terraces, tropical growths, camelia walks and much else covers 80 acres. Open to public and situated on A470 between Llandudno Junction and Llanrwst. A botanical treasure. Well worth a visit.

BODORGAN, Anglesey

2 miles SW of Aberffraw on A4080. Pleasant area of small villages, Hermon, Bethel and Malltraeth. Tefdraeth and St. Cadwalad churches well worth a visit.

BONTDDU, Gwynedd
On A469 between Barmouth and Llanelltyd and opposite Penrhyn Pool on the Mawddach. Hills above village famous for gold mines, which reached their peak in 1860's. Traditionally royal wedding rings have been made from Bontddu gold.

BORTH-Y-GEST, Gwynedd
SW of Porthmadog off the A487. Semi circular village around a bay. Sandy beaches, good bathing. Farmers reclaimed land in C18th but toxic marsh gas destroyed their crops. Site of the building of schooners in the C19th. Very attractive, unspoilt village.

BRENIG, Denbighshire
Off B4501 between Denbigh and Cerrigydrudion on Denbigh Moors. Bronze Age cairns, barrows, ritual monuments situated close to the Brenig Reservoir (Llyn Brenig, which is a recreation area). Archaelogical trail and visitors centre. Fishing and watersports.

BRYN CELLI DDU, Anglesey
Off A4080 between Llanfairpwell and Brynsiencyn. Neolithic chambered round cairn, 2000 to 1500 BC, considered to be best example of its kind in North Wales. Stone circle surrounds it.

BRYN EGLWYS, Gwynedd
S past Abergynolwyn village hall for 2 miles. Explore industrial archaeology of this former quarry village. Ruins of large, ornate houses and quarrymen's bunkhouses. Above reservoir.

BRYNKIR, Gwynedd
Woollen Mill. 12 miles S of Caernarfon on A487. Famed for wide and attractive range of traditional and modern patterns. Has been an active livestock centre.

BRYNSIENCYN, Anglesey (Pretty John's Hill)
On crossing Menai Bridge on A5 take first L turn at roundabout. Village in well-wooded surroundings but steeped in violent history. In AD 61 Roman soldiers crossed the Straits nearby and butchered the Druids. Tacitus wrote famous account of this event.

BUCKLEY, Flintshire (Bwcle)
On A549 21/2 miles from Mold. Noted as community which established reputation for brick making. Buckley bricks, together with ones from Ruabon, exported to many countries. Palace of King of Spain at Madrid made of Buckley bricks.

BULL BAY, Anglesey
Takes name from nearby inlet. On A5025 between Cemaes and Amlwch. Rocky coastal

walks and pleasant harbour. 18 hole golf course.

C

CADER IDRIS, Gwynedd
Name given to long range of mountains flanking S Side of Mawddach. Highest point Pen-y-Gadair. Subsidiary peaks Mynydd Moel and Llyn Cau. One of easiest ascents if from Abergynolwyn. Diarist Francis Kilvert made a C19th ascent. Folklore has it that if a poet spends a night on mountain he will become mad.

CAER DREWYN, Denbighshire. SJ 088444.
1 mile W of Corwen along A5. Iron Age hillfort on banks of the Dee. Prince Owain Gwynedd pitched his camp here when he was in ferocious combat with Henry II in 1165.

CAER GAI, Gwynedd
This Roman station is within close proximity of Llanuwchlyn, 1 1/2 miles E along A494. Permission to visit granted at local farm. Urns discovered here and also fragments of pottery. Votive slabs bear inscription.

CAERGWRLE, Flintshire
6 miles SE of Mold on A541. One interesting focal point; and early medieval hillfort built by Dafydd ap Gruffudd in 1277. Used as base for attacks on armies of Edward I when he was attempting to subjugate Welsh.

CAERHUN, Conwy
On B5106 S of Conwy on road form Glan Conwy to Llanrwst. Site of Roman Canovium. Traces of fort still visible. Medieval church at corner of site.

CAERNARFON, Gwynedd (Pop. 9,450)
Obtains name from Caer-yn-Arfon: fortified town in Arfon. Garrisoned during Roman

Caernarfon Castle

occupation and called Segontium. Castle circa 1283 very fine medieval fortress and, according to dubious version of history, birthplace of Edward II. Investiture of Charles Prince of Wales took place here in 1969. One of the best castles to visit.

CAER-Y-TWR, Anglesey
1 1/2 miles W of Holyhead at summit of Holyhead mountain. Hill fort which has utilised natural crags with dry stone ramparts. Wall walks completely encircle the fort; dates from the late pre-historic era.

CAERWYS, Flintshire
Small town on B5122 which connects A543 and A55. In C16th assumed great importance in cultural life of Wales when two Eisteddfods (poetry festivals) were held here. Entirely different kind of Eisteddfod revived in C18th.

CAPEL CURIG, Conwy
On A5 between Betws-y-Coed and Bethesda. In heart of Snowdonia. Good centre for mountaineers. Within short distance from Pen-y-Gwryd Hotel, at head of Nant Gwynant, which has incomparable associations with great climbers.

CAPEL GARMON, Conwy (Garmon's Chapel)
Peaceful upland village in Conwy valley some 3 miles above the busy A5. Best known as site of Neolithic burial chamber (1800 BC), S of village near farm called Tan-y-Coed. Major site with magnificent views of Snowdonia.

CARMEL HEAD, Anglesey (Trwyn y Cader)
Large headland in N part of island now owned by National Trust. Energetic walkers will be rewarded with magnificent coastal views. Many walkers begin walk at Mynachdy, 1 mile from Llanfairynghonwy and hike the whole distance to Church Bay further along coast in Holyhead direction. Divides W from N coast.

CARNEDD RANGE, Conwy
Range of mountains within Snowdonia National Park situated between Capel Curig and Bethesda. Carnedd Llewelyn (1000,62 ft.) and Carnedd Dafydd (1000, 27 ft.). Uncertain name derivation but could be connected with retreat of two unfortunate last princes of Wales.

CARROG, Denbighshire
On A5 3 1/2 miles out of Corwen in direction of Llangollen. On journey towards Llangollen turn L, proceed until you cross C17th bridge, and bear L again. Terminus of Llangollen Steam Railway. Mound of Owain Glyndwr close to Dee.

CASTELL CIDWM, Gwynedd (Wolf's Castle)
At N end of Cwellyn Lake on Caernarfon-Beddgelert A4085 road. Situated at N end of Llyn Cwellyn. Early British fort once held by robber chief who allegedly murdered a brother of Roman emperor Constantine.

Castell DINAS BRAN, Denbighshire
Situated high above Llangollen are ruins of C13th castle on site where there are traces of Iron hill fort. Has had violent and chequered history in Welsh/English invasions. If on foot take footpath from Llangollen beside garage near N end of bridge. Cross canal by road bridge and take path up brick steps close to school. Well signposted from there on.

CASTELL-Y-BERE, Gwynedd
7 miles S of Dolgellau off B4405 nr Abergynolwyn. Ruins of once important fortification begun by Llewelyn the Great in 1221. Surrendered to English in 1283. Set in pastoral surroundings in Dysynni Valley.

CEFN MAWR, Wrexham (Large Cave)
Situated on A483 between Llangollen and Wrexham. Traditionally an industrial area, and the base for a chemical plant. Close by Telford's aqueduct spans the Dee. Built 1797 and regarded as one of wonders of its period (127ft).

CEFN MERIADOG, Conwy (Meriadog's Cave)
5 miles E of St. Asaph in Elwy Valley. Take B5381 from St. Asaph and turn L before S bend. Elegant church built of local stone. In limestone gorge is ruined well chapel. Ffynnon Fair (See St. Mary's Well). Nearby Pontnewydd cave excavated in recent years and now of international archaelogical importance. Artefacts discovered dating from Paleolithic and Neolithic periods.

CEIRIOG VALLEY, Wrexham (Dyffryn Ceiriog)
Take B4500 at Chirk down scenic tree-lined road, following the river Ceiriog into the Berwyn hills. Tomen-y-Meirw, pre-historic burial mound above valley. Outside a farmhouse, Pont-y-Mebion, is memorial to great C17th Welsh poet Huw Morris. George Borrow came here in 1854 to seek out his stone chair as an act of homage. See Glyn Ceiriog.

CEMLYN BAY, Anglesey
On A5025 and consists of sheltered lagoon, home of many water birds. Very popular with ornithologists.

CEMMAES, BAY, Anglesey
Most northerly village in Wales, on A5025 between Valley and Amlwch. Encloses small harbour. Nearby is Wylfa Head Nuclear Power Station, open to visitors during Summer months. Incorporates excellent visitors' centre.

CERRIGYDRUDION, Conwy (Stones of the Daring Ones)
9 miles W of Corwen on A5. Village located within area known as Hiraethog. Much sheep farming. Traditionally an area of local culture among common people. Bell turret on church a memorial to local men who died in 2nd World War.

CEUNANT MAWR, Llanberis, Gwynedd
Take lane on left of church. After 600 yards follow signposted path on right. Vantage point on top of narrow ravine where Arddu river plunges for 120ft. Good views of comings and goings of Snowdon Mountain Railway trains.

CILCAIN, Flintshire
11/2 miles off A541 W of Mold on Denbigh road. Unspoiled village. Church has angular hammer beams which came from Basingwerk Abbey. Good access point for walking on Clwydian range.

CHIRK, Wrexham
Border village on A5, 5 miles E of Llangollen. Here River Ceiriog joins Dee. Main interest focused on Chirk Castle mile W of village. National Trust property. Open April-late Sept. Magnificent parkland.

CLOCAENOG, Denbighshire
Approached along B5105 from A5 at Cerrigydrudion. This sheep-farming area is now mostly owned by Forestry Commission and they have opened up parts of it as recreation areas for visitors. Popular with picnickers.

CLOGWYN DU'R ARDDU, Gwynedd OS Ref. Sh 599556
Best known rock climbing area on Snowdon, known affectionately as 'Cloggie'. Extends from Llyn Du'r Arddu to join W ridge off Snowdon leading into Cwm Brwynog. Divided into 8 main climbing areas, the most popular being the East Buttress.

CLWYD RIVER, Denbighshire (Afon Clwyd)
Flows 30 miles from source near Melin-y-Wig through Vale of Clwyd to Rhuddlanwhere it becomes tidal before joining sea at Rhyl. Much extolled by literary tourists and popular with anglers.

CLWYD VALLEY, Denbighshire (Dyffryn Clwyd)
Extensive fertile valley, and best known example in Britain of rift valley. In glacial period it emerged as a depression between 2 faults. Underground is a large artesian lake. Principal towns are Ruthin and Denbigh. Visitors will also find a number of charming villages.

CLEWEDOG, Wrexham
On A483, it comprises among its attractions an adventure trail, Minera lead mines and a country park. Also the Bersham Iron works and Erddig hall, Kings Mill visitor centre and Farmworld.

CLYNNOG, FAWR, Gwynedd (Place of Holy Trees)
Small village between Nefyn and Caernarfon with surprisingly large Gothic church, on site with associations with St. Beuno (C7th). His well may be seen on roadside W of

church. Resting place for pilgrims to Bardsey.

COED-Y-BRENIN, Gwynedd
Best approached form Llanelltyd on A470. Forest park planted in honour of George V. Nature trails and visitors' centre. In earlier times gold mines could be found in the area.

COLWYN BAY, Conwy (Pop. 28,150)
Town now by-passed by A55, and when travelling from Abergele a stunning sweep of bay is unexpectedly revealed. Railway separates town from sea. In 1866 only one house stood where town has now grown. Pwllycrochan Hall was turned into a hotel and railway station was built to serve it. Resort evolved around station. Eirias Park, noted leisure centre. Dinosaur World and Welsh Mountain Zoo. Civic offices of Conwy County located here. The zoo is well worth a family visit.

CONNAH'S QUAY, Flintshire
Important town in maritime history of NE Wales situated on A548 between Flint and Shotton. Town takes name from C19th industrial agent. Became important centre of export. Bricks from nearby Buckley sent abroad. In 1900 200,000 tons a year were being handled here.

CONWY
New county which came into being as a result of the reorganisation of County boundaries in 1995. Extending from Kinmel Bay, near Rhyl, to the north, it embraces Blaenau Ffestiniog in the south. Other Conwy communities include Colwyn Bay, Llandudno, Penmaenmarrw, Llanfihangel Glyn Myfyr and Llanefydd. Population: 109,006. Area: 112,995 hectares. Civic offices at Colwyn Bay.

CONWY, Conwy (Pop. 12,000)
On A55 W of Llandudno Junction. Founded by Maelgwyn Gwynedd circa 581. Fine example of Edwardian walled town (1288). Castle figured prominently in both medieval history and in C16th Civil War. Plas Mawr, built in Elizabethan times, oldest surviving town house in Britain. Open to public. On quayside look out for 'Smallest House in Britain'. Charlotte Bronte spent her honeymoon here. Very good visitors' centre.

CONWY VALLEY (Dyffryn Conwy)
River carved its way through rock fault before Ice Age. Glaciers flowed down its course deepening valley floor, making wide, flat fertile bottom which you see today. Extensive and beautiful region steeped in historical events of importance and much extolled by Wales Tourist Board, as visit to Conwy Visitor Centre will reveal.

CONWY VALLEY RAILWAY
Another of the small railways of North Wales which runs from a terminus at Betws-y-Coed. Close to the main line railway station. Access by car is from the high street, opposite a hotel. Result of the enterprise of Colin Cartwright, a railway enthusiast. Former railway carriage houses a cafe. The short ride on miniature carriages behind steam

engines takes passengers through beautifully-wooded landscape. Steam locomotive museum.

CONWY FALLS, Conwy
Situated below the A5 1 miles from Betws-y-Coed as you approach from direction of Corwen. Entrance on payment through turnstile close to the Conwy Falls Cafe.

CONWY LAKE, Conwy (Llyn Conwy)
Off B4407 between Ysbyty Ifan and Ffestiniog. Easy approach on foot from road. High on moorland plateau of Mignient. Occupies 100 acres at height of 1,488 ft. Source of river Conwy. Very popular with salmon poachers during last century.

CONWY RIVER (Afon Conwy)
Rises in Llyn Conwy, small lake in uplands of Migneint area, which joins Mynydd Hiraethog to Snowdonia. After flowing S for a mile it turns NE and flows into the valley. From its source to the sea it travels 23 miles.

CORRIS, Gwynedd
Two separate villages, Coris Uchaf and Corris, 3/4 mile apart on A487 between Dolgellau and Machynlleth. Located in well-wooded valley and traditionally associated with slate quarrying. Between two villages is Corris Craft Centre where craft workers can be seen at work. On site is King Arthur's Labyrinth, tunnels and caverns under hillside where visitors can explore the Arthurian world. Open April-Oct.

CORWEN, Denbighshire (Cor-sacred place Maen-stone) (Pop. 1,500)
On A5 10 miles W of Llangollen. Traditionally a market town. Owain Glyndŵr has strong associations with area and hotel is named after him. Church dedicated to St. Sulien well worth a visit. Interesting grave inscriptions.

COWLYD LAKE, Conwy (Llyn Cowlyd)
Approached on foot by rough track above Trefriw off B5106. Can be reached by road. Contains largest trout in Wales and lake is deepest in North Wales. Covers 269 acres at height of 1,200 ft. Legend has it that a water bull lives in its depths.

CNICHT, Gwynedd
Name derives from Saxon word for knight, as peak resembles armed knight in shape. Approach village of Croesor on A496 from Ffestiniog or B4485 and B4410 from Beddgelert. Path begins to the left of chapel at Croesor. Has been compared to Matterhorn (2,265 ft.).

CRAFNANT LAKE, Conwy (Llyn Crafnant)
Situated in Carneddau group of mountains 602 ft. up. Covers 52 acres. Dam built 1874, gives lake volume of 430,000 cubic metres, but no longer provides domestic water. Excellent fishing. Craf is Welsh for garlic, which is abundant here in early Spring. Approach on B5106 between Betws-y-Coed and Conwy and take minor road.

CRIB GOCH, Gwynedd
Eastern ridge of Snowdon massif (3,230 ft.) With Y Lliwedd it is often known as the 'Snowdon Horseshoe'. Often cited as finest ridge walk in Britain.

CRICCIETH, Gwynedd (The Sorrowful Rock) (Pop. 1,618)
On A497 between Porthmadog and Pwllheli. Castle (1230) built by Welsh. In 1282 Edward I captured it. Reclaimed for Welsh by Owain Glyndŵr 1404. Stands on prominent headland overlooking Cardigan Bay. Lloyd George has strong associations with the area (See Llanystumdwy). A very attractive, unspoilt village; well-known for its ice cream.

CROESOR, Gwynedd
Take single track minor road off the A4485 Beddgelert-Penrhyndeudraeth road. If travelling towards Beddgelert turn R under archway near impressive house called Plas Brondanwg, once home of architect Clough Williams Ellis. Proceed for over 3 miles to hamlet, economy of which once depended on slate. Bob Owen, Croesor, was well known figure due to his remarkable self-education. Valley has provided homes for many writers and artists.

CWELLYN LAKE, Gwynedd (Llyn Cwellyn)
Approached on A4085, half-way between Caernarfon and Beddgelert. Accessible for motor vehicles. Deep lake covering 215 acres at height of 463 ft. Surrounded by conifer forests which make it reminiscent of Norwegian locales. No swimming. Char in depths.

CWM BYCHAN, Gwynedd
Lake in remote area in Rhiniog mountains. Covers 25 acres and is 505 ft. above sea level. On its shores the 1937 film *The Drum* was made. Nearby are 'Roman Steps' a paved mountain path. White goats of Rhinogs may be seen by the fortunate. Thomas Pennant C18th antiquarian and scholar, describes area in *Tours in Wales*.

CWM NANTCOL, Gwynedd
4 miles W of Llanbedr off A496 Harlech-Barmouth road. Gradually ascends valley of Atro river with its tributary Cwmnancol. Part of Rhinog Nature Reserve. Very wild area of heather, boulders and very rough walking. Evidence of manganese mining in the area.

CWM Y STRADLYN LAKE, Gwynedd (Llyn Cwm-y-Stradlyn) GR 5644
Accessible by motor car. Rather gloomy, and covering 98 acres at height of 642 ft. up. Dangerous former quarry workings at its head. Off the A487 in Dolbenmaen, north of Porthmadog.

CYNFAL FALLS, Gwynedd
21/2 miles east of Llan Ffestiniog on B4391. Waterfall consists of six cataracts in sheer-sided treeless rocky gorge. 300 ft. high. Vista of Porthmadog and Cardigan Bay.
CYNFAL RIVER, Gwynedd (Afon Cynfal)
Flows under A470 between Ffestiniog and Trawsfynydd. On banks of this river Blodeuwedd and her lover plotted the bizarre death of of Lleu in *The Mabinogion*.

CYMER ABBEY, Gwynedd
On E bank of Mawddach 1 miles from Dolgellau facing village of Llanelltyd. Cistercian abbey founded 1198 by Llewelyn the Great. Elegant standing walls and delicate arches and nave remain.

D

DEE River
Over 90 miles it flows from source in Berwyn Hills, passing through Bala Lake and the Vale of Llangollen before eventually ending its journey in border country near Chester and flowing into the Dee Estuary. Much folklore about the river.

DEGANWY, Conwy (Pop. 2,818)
On A546 between Llandudno Junction and Llandudno. Only resort on N. Wales coast facing S. Deganwy Castle originally built by Maelgwyn Gwynedd in C6th. Rebuilt several times, but destroyed by Llewelyn ap Gruffydd in 1262.

DENBIGHSHIRE
County is situated in NE of Wales; came into being in its present form in 1995. Communities include Denbigh, Ruthin, Corwen, Llangollen, St. Asaph, Rhyl, Prestatyn and Bodfari. The county offices are located in Ruthin. The old county of Denbigh — before it was made part of the Clwyd — dated back to the C16th.

DENBIGH, Denbighshire (Pop. 10,000)
Name derivation derived from Celtic dounon-enclosed place and bach-small. Approach from coast on A525 and from Pentrefoelas on 548. Town dominated by Edwardian castle, built by Henry de Lacy in 1281. Best approached up steep Bull Lane to left of main post office in town square. Whitchurch (Eglwyswen) on Whitchurch Road; Denbigh Abbey off Rhyl Road also worth a visit. Birthplace of H. M. Stanley ("Dr. Livingstone I presume"). Dr. Johnson visited the area, marked by a monument beside the Ystrad river. The poet, Gerard Manley Hopkins visited the castle when he lived nearby in Tremeirchion in the 1870's. When the poet *Colerdge* visited Denbigh Castle in 1794 he claimed that "... it surpasses everything I could have conceived... I wandered there an hour-and-a-half".

DERWEN, Denbighshire
From Ruthin take A494. After 7 miles take R turn at Bryn Saith Marchog. Most notable feature is churchyard cross, best preserved in Vale of Clwyd. Church retains its C15th rood and loft.

DEVIL'S KITCHEN, Gwynedd (Twll Ddu)
In Glyder area of Snowdonia between A5 and A4086. Tall, black chimney formed in rock. Name derives from fact that water gurgles and foams as it crashes down a height

of several hundred feet.

DINAS DINLLE, Gwynedd (fort of Lleu)
Off A499 road between Clynnog Fawr and Caernarfon. Travelling from Caernarfon look for sign on R and take minor road. Area rich in myth and history and associated with ancient story of Blodeuwedd, a lady made of flowers, in *The Mabinogion*. Excavations reveal that Romans occupied area in C2nd AD.

DINAS EMRYS, Gwynedd
On A498 between Beddgelert and Nant Gwynant. Important Iron Age site. Also ruins of C12th keep. Associations with Ambrosius, Roman general whose British name was Emrys. C5th connections with Vortigern and Merlin.

DINAS LAKE, Gwynedd (Llyn Dinas) GR6149
Shallow lake covering 60 acres and 177 ft. above sea level. Part of the Wyddfa group from which a river flows down to sea. Forty years ago Ingrid Bergman film *Inn of the Sixth Happiness* made on location in the area. Between Capel Curig and Beddgelert. Marvellous scenery.

DIN LLIGWY, Anglesey
From Amlwch take B5052 S for 7 miles to Llanallgo. Signpost at roundabout. Well preserved and important Iron Age site covering 1/2 acre. Contains remains of fortified residence constructed of large roughly shaped stones.

DIWAUNYDD LAKES, Conwy GR6856
Two hourglass shaped lakes between Mynydd Cribau and Moel Siabod, SE of Capel Curig on A5. Once belonged to Cobden's Hotel at Capel Curig. They cover 19 acres and 13 acres respectively and are 1,207 ft. up.

DINORWIC QUARRIES, Gwynedd
E of Caernarfon on A4086 in Llanberis. Quarries closed in 1969, but on the site are well preserved workshops, old machinery and tools. Is now Welsh Slate Museum.

DOLBADARN CASTLE, Gwynedd
Close to N end of Llyn Peris in Llanberis. Fortress of Welsh princes. Owen Goch imprisoned here because of revolt against brother Llywelyn ap Iorweth. In 1402 Lord Grey of Ruthin imprisoned here by Owain Glyndŵr and released when ransom of 10,000 marks was paid.

DOLBENMAEN, Gwynedd
Crossroads village off Caernarfon-Tremadog road (A487). Associations with *The Mabinogion* involving Gwydion and sacred pigs of Pryderi.

DOLGARROG, Conwy
Village on B5106 in Conwy Valley between Llanrwst and Conwy. In 1907 the Aluminium Corporation built factory and power station producing 10,000 kilowatts of

power from Llyn Eigau and Llyn Cowlyd.

DOLGELLAU, Gwynedd (Pop. 2,680)
Town on A496 between Barmouth and Machynlleth; can be reached from Bala on A494. Stands on River Wnion, main tributary of Mawddach. Greystone buildings in neat narrow streets with small squares. Figured prominently in Glyndŵr rebellion and he held last Welsh parliament here in 104 when he made famous treaty with Charles VI of France. Important area for Quakers in Welsh history. When he dined at an inn in 1872 *Francis Kilvert* commented that "... into the soup the cook had upset both the salt cellar and the pepper pot". He was much taken by a girl whom he saw in the town. She had "... eyes singularly lovely, the sweetest saddest most weary and most patient eyes I ever saw".

DOLGOCH FALLS, Gwynedd
2 miles N of Tywyn. Turn from A493 into B4405 and continue for 2 1/2 miles. Falls descend through Nant Dol-Goch to river Fathew below. Good paths and fine views.

DOLWYDDELAN, Conwy
Village on A470 SW of Betws-y-Coed. Once a quarrying community. C16th church with Gothic rood screen.

DOLWYDDELAN CASTLE, Gwynedd
Clearly visible from A470 SW of Betws-y-Coed at head of Lledr valley. Presumed birthplace of Llewelyn the Great (1173) and rebuilt following English conquest in 1283. Painted and written about in verse by Turner. Open throughout year. The road over to Blaenau Ffestiniog is called Crimea.

DOVEY, River, Gwynedd (Afon Dyfi)
A very good example of a river acting as a boundary, in this case between Gwynedd and Ceredigion. It has its source on the mountainous region known as Aran Mawddwy (905 ft.). Legend relates how the beautiful child, and future poet, Taliesin was found in a coracle on the river.

DULYN LAKE, Conwy (Llyn Dulan) GR 6624
Up a rough track from Dolgarrog on B5106 Conwy-Llanrwst road. Only approachable on foot. Remote, black crater-like lake overshadowed by Craig Dulyn. 33 acres and 55 ft. deep, 1,747 ft. up. Sometimes referred to as 'the aircrafts graveyard' due to the fact that 20 planes have crashed in this vicinity during the last war.

DWYFOR, River, Gwynedd
Has source near Cwm Trwsgol, close to edge of Beddgelert Forest and ends on coastal area of Llŷn between Llanystumdwy and Pwllheli where it joins sea at Cardigan Bay. David Lloyd George is buried on its banks.

DYFFRYN ARDUDWY, Gwynedd (Vale of Ardudwy)
Takes name from region of Ardudwy. Village on A496 between Harlech and Barmouth situated between Harlech Dome and sea. Two burial chambers behind school. Church has

stone bearing inscriptions so ancient that they seem to pre-date Christianity.

DYFFRYN BURIAL CHAMBERS, Gwynedd
5 miles S of Harlech on A496 to village of Dyffryn Ardudwy. 2 easily accessible chambers from Neolithic period. They are characteristic of ones found in Ireland and probably offer proof of early sea voyages between N Wales and Ireland at that time.

DYSERTH, Denbighshire
Name derived drom diserth which means a wilderness. 31/2 miles from Rhyl. Take A526 towards Rhuddlan, turn L at roundabout and follow signposting. 40ft. waterfall formed by stream from St. Asaph's Well (Ffynnon Asaph) in adjoining parish of Cwm. Castle once stood on promontory 1/2 mile from village.

DYWARCHEN LAKE (Llyn y Dywarchen) GR 5653
Small lake above Rhyd Ddu covering 40 acres at height of 767 ft. Had appeal for naturalists and tourists because it had a floating peat island. First recorded by Gerald of Wales in 1188. On the high, twisting road between Rhyd Ddu and Nantlle.

E

EDNO LAKE, Conwy (Llyn Edno) GR 6649
Can be reached on the D470 S of Betws-y-Coed. It covers 10 acres and is 1,797 ft. up. Cannibal trout found here. Charles Kingsley, the writer, found some when he came here in C19th. Surrounded by rock and heather.

EGLWYSEG ROCKS, Denbighshire
Range of limestone cliffs running along N side of Vale of Llangollen, rising to 1,648 ft. From ridge is extensive view extending to Shropshire in one direction and Snowdonia in the other.

ELISEG'S PILLAR, Denbighshire. SJ 202445
On A542 between Ruthin and Llangollen in area known as "Horseshoe Pass" and quite close to Valle Crucis Abbey. C9th memorial stone and erected before Abbey was founded. Eliseg was king of Powys.

ELSI LAKE, Conwy (Llyn Elsi) GR7855
Footpath from St. Mary's Church, Betws-y-Coed. Before it was transformed into a reservoir it consisted of two lakes. It now covers 26 acres. Originally one of the lakes was called Enoc, the name of a Welsh chieftain who had his hand cut off when he was caught on the wrong side of Offa's Dyke. Painter and book illustrator Walter Crane took the lakes as his subject when he visited around 1900.

ELWY RIVER (Afon Elwy)
Has source in Denbighshire uplands and flows into the limestone valley of same name before proceeding to St. Asaph to join the river Clwyd. Together they join sea at Rhyl.

Source on Denbigh Moors.

ELWY VALLEY, Denbighshire/Conwy (Dyffryn Elwy)
Well wooded valley cut in carboniferous limestone gorge. In the Cefnmeiriadog area of valley important pre-historic discoveries have been made. Valley written of by Gerard Manley Hopkins in his well-known poem *In the Valley Of The Elwy.*

ERBISTOCK, Wrexham
Turn off A5069 at Overton. Village lies in loop of Dee before it flows under Overton Bridge. Attractive church and C17th Boat Inn. Erbistock mill and weir can be seen from road.

ERDDIG, Wrexham
On A483 S of Wrexham. Well signposted. Stately home now owned by National Trust. 'Upstairs, downstairs' nature of house is main feature of interest. Built 1687 and home of Yorke family for centuries until last heir died with no progeny in nineteen-eighties. Magnificent garden.

EWLOE CASTLE, Flintshire
On A55 between Northop and Hawarden 10 miles SE of Holywell. Ruins obscured by woodland. Welsh castle following victory by forces of Owain Glyndŵr. Impressive 'Welsh tower'.

F

FAIRBOURNE, Gwynedd
Village on level land facing Barmouth across tip of Mawddach estuary. 1 mile off A493. Golf course and good bathing. Fairbourne Railway was laid to transport building materials for construction of bridge over Mawddach in 1867. Now tourist attraction. The railway has narrowest gauge in Wales (121/4 inches).

FAIRBOURNE RAILWAY, Gwynedd
50 yards from main line station. Was old horse-drawn tramway carrying slate from Friog quarry to Penrhyn Point. Now last 2 miles of track utilised by miniature railway. Two stations en route — Beach Halt and Passing Loop.

FAIRY GLEN, Conwy
Just before junction of A5 and A470 in Conwy Valley between Dolwyddelan and Betws-y-Coed. Water swirls through a deep chasm, overhung with trees. See Betws-y-Coed. Enter by payment at gate.

FFESTINIOG RAILWAY, Gwynedd
Station at Porthmadog. Narrow gauge railway (1836) built to link harbour at Porthmadog to Ffestiniog Slate Quarry. Visitors can travel 10 miles through beautiful countryside.

Unique 1' 11½" (two foot gauge). One of the world's finest railways. Travels through Penrhyndendraeth to Blaenau Ffestiniog.

FFESTINIOG VALLEY, Gwynedd (Afon Ffestiniog)
Lush, well wooded, steep-sided valley. River Cyntaf meanders through it. Incorporates parts of National Park. Much extolled by C19th writers, such as Thomas Love Peacock.

FLINTSHIRE
The county is situated in NE Wales, close to the English border, and came into being in its present form in 1995. Communities include Flint, Holywell, Mold, Connah's Quay, and Caerwys. The county offices are located at Mold.

FLINT, Flintshire. (Pop. 15,250)
On A548 coast road between Connah's Quay and Holywell. Castle built by Edward I in 1275, and Shakespeare set short sequence of *Richard II* there. Borough town dating from Middle Ages which gave its name to the original Flintshire county.

FFRAW RIVER, Anglesey (Afon Ffraw) On A4080 Newborough-Rhosneigr road. Little river flowing into enormous stretches of sand at the coat. Hump-backed bridge crosses it at Aberffraw. See Aberffraw.

FRONGOCH, Gwynedd (Red Hillside)
Hamlet on A212 between Bala and Trawsfynydd. Welsh whiskey brewed here in C19th. During First World War there was internment camp here in which Irish rebels were incarcerated. During captivity they were able to hatch political plots to secure freedom of Ireland. Became known as 'the university of revolution'.

FYDDLYN COVE, Anglesey
Walk from Church Bay on footpath which begins by ascending high above the beach and keep walking northwards over Carmel Head until you arrive at Mynachdy, 1 mile from Llanfairynhonwy. At cove is island separated from mainland by narrow chasm protecting it. Used by Vikings as base when they launched attack on Penmon Priory. See Carmel Head.

FFYNNON CASEG, Gwynedd (The Mares Well)
On A5 Bethesda-Capel Curig road between Yr Elen and Carnedd Llewelyn. Tradition has it that wild ponies come here in Spring to give birth.

FFYNNONGROEW, Flintshire
By-passed by A548 between Prestatyn and Flint. Village close to Point of Ayr Colliery which operated for 130 years before closure in 1996. Played some role in maritime history of area in late C19th.
FFYNNON LLOER LAKE, Gwynedd (Llyn Ffynnon Lloer) GR6662
The name means 'The Well of the Moon' and it is approached by foot. It is located in the southern valleys of the Carnedds and at a height of 2,255ft. the highest crater lake in

Snowdonia. Covers 6 acres.

G

GARNFADRYN, Gwynedd
At end of Llŷn peninsular off B4413 and well signposted. Hill fort near Porth Oer. Part of Heritage Coastline.

GEGIN FAWR, Aberdaron, Gwynedd (Big Kitchen)
Built in 1300 and has served as resting place for pilgrims to Bardsey. At some point was used as a courthouse while a prison and gallows stood nearby. Now a cafe.

GEIRIONYDD LAKE, Llanrwst (llyn Geirionydd) GR 7660
Can be approached from the old church at Llanrhychwyn above Betws-y-Coed. Covering an area of 45 acres, it has associations with native poets and hymn writers. A number of Eisteddfodau were held on its shores. Until recent years locals have believed the lake poisoned.

GLAN CONWY, Conwy (Glan-edge)
On A470 Conwy-Llanrwst road. Was busy small port in earlier times and can be seen as frontier between rural valley and urbanised stretch of coastline. Welsh name Llansanffraid.

GLAS LAKE (Llyn Glas) GR 6155
Approach on foot at N ridge of Crib Goch. Lies 2,300 ft. up and covers 1 acre. Folklore relates how Merlin hid the golden throne of Britain here. William Bingley,C19th botanist, called it "the speckled pool".

GLASLYN LAKE, Gwynedd (Llyn Glaslyn)
Close to the summit of Snowdon: 1,970 ft. up and covers 18 acres. The haunt of demons according to the prolific local folklore which is associated with it, and antiquarian Edward Llwyd recorded some of these.

GLASLYN RIVER (Afon Glaslyn)
Has source on Yr Aran (747). Part of previous river area is now estuary and much land was reclaimed from sea by William Madocks early in C19th. One of the most picturesque rivers in Wales. Drive along it from Beddgelent to Porthmadog; draw in to lay-bys and walk the river-bank. Site of track of the Highland Railway; see the tunnels in the rock.

GLYNDFYRDWY, Denbighshire (Valley of the water of the Dee)
On A5 between Llangollen and Corwen. Station here reopened by the Llangollen Steam Railway Society. Strong links with Owain Glyndwr who had a house near the river on a manmade mound.

GLYDER MOUNTAINS
Located between Bangor and Capel Curig on the A5 and the 4086 Llanberis - Pen-y-Gwryd road. Group of mountains looking over narrow valley of Snowdonia range with two predominant points — Glyder Fach and Glyder Mawr.

GREAT ORME, Llandudno
Take A470 from Llandudno Junction. Cable car and tramway run to summit. St. Tudno's is a much restored medieval church. Orme was fertile area for copper mining in Roman times and workings have now been excavated and are open to public. A feature of the landscape of Llandudno, an elegant seaside town created on virgin land (owned by the Mostyn family) in the mid C19th.

GWYDIR CASTLE, Llanrwst, Conwy
On outskirts of town off B5106, Gwydir is stately Elizabethan house. Seat of Wynn family from early C16th until recent times. Tree in garden commemorates marriage of Charles I. Privately owned but with access to public.

GWYDYR FOREST TRAIL, Conwy GR 756576
Above the Ugly House on A5, 3 miles W of Betws-y-Coed. Forestry Commission. Information sheet available. A walk for all seasons, by arrangement.

GWYNANT LAKE, Gwynedd (Llyn Gwynant) GR 6154
Between Capel Curig and Beddgelert. Covers 18 acres and is 1,970 ft. up. In C19th was known as "The Green Lake". Situated beneath E face of Snowdon with depth of 127ft. At one time it was believed to be bottomless. There are reports of fairies having been seen here. Shepherd fed them, and when he returned home discovered silver coin in payment.

GWYNEDD
Ancient county in NW Wales. Named Gwynedd in C6th. Name derived from the Venedotae tribe. Further subdivisions in the Middle Ages. The evolution of the county boundaries which existed up to 1995 were imposed by Edward I in 1284. But in 1995 a large portion of northern Gwynedd became a part of the new county of Conwy under county reorganisation. Communities include Caernarfon, Porthmadog, Criccieth, Aberdaron, Penrhyndeudraeth, Barmouth, Dolgellau, and Tywyn.

GWYTHERIN, Conwy
From Abergele take A548 towards Llanrwst. After 8 miles take A544 at Llanfair TH. After 4 miles take B5384 R at Llansannan. Follow signposting. In churchyard of this remote village is a row of standing stones which could be C5th. St. Winifred reputed to have lived as a nun here and fate of her mortal remains provides ingenious plot in Ellis Peter's first Brother Cadfael novel *A Morbid Taste for Bones*.

H

HAPPY VALLEY, Llandudno
Popular gardens close to Great Orme. In the Fifties it was popular venue of live Summer entertainment, inc. Alex Munroe Show. Fine sea views.

HARLECH, Gwynedd (Beautiful Rock) (Pop. 1,676)
Small town on B4573 between Maentwrog and Barmouth. Made world famous by song *'Men of Harlech'*. Immensely impressive castle; one of Edward I's ring of fortresses built to facilitate his colonisation of Wales. Site of castle in much earlier times known as Twr Bronwen, Bronwen's Tower, after the tragic story of this ill-fated woman recounted in *The Mabiogion*. Royal St. David's Golf Course much commended. Coleg Harlech, residential adult education college, founded 1927.

HARLECH DOME, Gwynedd
Wonderful mountain road skirts this stunning upland area of Ardudwy, the oldest mountain mass in Wales. Historic relics, wooded valleys, lakes.

HANMER and PENLEY, Wrexham
Two twin villages 2 miles apart in lowland plain near Ruabon. 9 miles from Wrexham on A539. Hanmer Mere, a well-frequented beauty spot.

HAWARDEN, Flintshire (Benarlag)
On A556 6 miles W of Chester. Village guarded route into N. Wales at past times of historical conflict. Old castle built in Norman times and rebuilt C13th. Hawarden Castle, home of William Gladstone; family are commemorated in parish church. St. Deiniol's Residential Library, next to church, is a source of local information.

HOLYWELL, Flintshire (Treffynnon)
Homestead of well is the derivation of the name. Site of St. Winifrede's Well, noted in the curing of bodily ailments. Gothic building covers spring and it is reputed to have been built by Margaret Beaufort, mother of Henry VII, to replace an earlier structure. Often referred to as 'the Lourdes of Wales'. Could be the source of references to a 'bath' in Shakespeare's Sonnets. "...a bath and healthful remedy for men diseased... I came there for cure". (S.154).

HELL'S MOUTH, Gwynedd
Striking name for an area of coastline on tip on Llŷn, owned by National Trust, between Braich-y-Pwll and Mynydd Cilan. Sometimes referred to as the 'Lands End' of Wales.

HENLLAN, Denbighshire (Old Church)
Take B5382 from Denbigh for 2¹/₂ miles. Village has unusual feature in that the church and bell tower are separate. Birthplace of great C16th polymath Humphrey Llwyd. Llindir Inn dates from C13th and is reputed to be haunted by ghost of 'woman in white'.

HOLT, Wrexham
On A534 NW of Wrexham. Was medieval borough built around castle at end of C13th. Sandstone bridge from early C15th links it to Farndon in Cheshire. In 1880's the writer H. G. Wells spent some time on the teaching staff of the Holt Academy. See his *Experiment in Autobiography.*

HOLYHEAD, Anglesey (Caer Gybi)
Reached by A5. Terminal for ferry sailings to Ireland and very much a port town. Parish church of St. Gybi inside late Roman fort. Roman wall. Railway opened 1850 and a breakwater completed 1873. Jonathan Swift wrote very jaundiced comments on town.

HOLYHEAD MOUNTAIN, Anglesey (Mynydd Cear Gybi)
Highest point on Anglesey at 720 ft. Impressive hill fort occupied down to Roman times. South Stack lighthouse. Elan Tower birdwatching point. Prehistoric hut circles.

HOLY ISLAND
A causeway over which the A5 runs, connects the island of Anglesey with this smaller island, but they are both referred to as Anglesey. St. Gybi founded church here C6th hence old name Ynys Gybi. See Holyhead.

HORSESHOE PASS, Denbighshire
On A542 between Ruthin and Llangollen. So named because mountainous road has wide curve. This remote area is frequently impassable due to adverse weather during Winter months. See Valle Crucis. A dramatic scenic drive. Stop and admire the heather and gorse in late Summer.

IDWAL SLABS
Between the Llanberis Pass and the A5 Capel Curig-Bangor road. Unusual flora, some unique to area. Widely used by climbers as training area. A huge, smooth, sloping rock, with long cracks.

K

KENDRICK'S CAVE, Conway
Situated on Great Orme, Llandudno; some of earliest pre-historic artefacts in Gwynedd have been discovered here. Evidence of Paleolithic occupation. No access to public.

KINMEL PARK (Kinmel Hall). St. George, Bodelwyddan, Denbighshire.
Entrance through gateway in long wall on hillside near Bodelwyddian Castle. Originally built 1791-1802 by Edward Hughes, who made a fortune out of copper at Parrys Mountain, Anglesey. Extensions through C19th reflect countryhouse styles: the brick exterior with stone dressings owes much to Wren and Hampton Court. The E front comprises 15 bays, extending 190 feet. The ballroom is 60 ft. long. An Entrance Lodge to the

above sits aside the A55 at Bodelwyddan, Bodelwyddan is Queen Anne style; designed by Nesfield, 1868. A magnificent chimney-piece with heraldic enbems of Welsh noble families occupies the diningroom of Kinmel Manor, Abergele, now a hotel; this was originally in the entrance hallway of Kinmel Hall.

L

LEETE WALK, Flintshire
Walk extending from Rhydymwyn on A541 Denbigh-Mold road to Loggerheads. Lead mining area in the past. Mendelssohn stayed at nearby Coed Ddu in 1829 and composed three short pieces here. Plaque in Rhydymwyn commemorates his visits and that of Charles Kingsley.

LLAGI LAKE, Gwynedd (Llyn Llagi) GR6448
Approached on B4085 between Porthmadog and Beddgelert and covering 8 acres at a height of 1,238. Remains of old settlement on NW shore, which could be a crannog or artificial island. Occupied by Beaker People. Many tales of fairies. Good trout fishing.

LLANALLGO, Anglesey
Small parish in NE of island. Churchyard contains graves of 140 who lost lives when 'Royal Charter' was wrecked off nearby coast in 1859. Dickens stayed at rectory and wrote of tragedy in *The Uncommercial Traveller.*

LLANARMON-YN-IÂL, Denbighshire
Situated between Corwen and Hawarden on A494. Village in limestone terrain below Clwydian range on Wrexham side. Iâl is Welsh for cultivated area and name was adopted by local family as surname, best-known member being Elihu Yale, benefactor of Yale University, U.S.A. (see Wrexham).

LLANASA, Flintshire
Name probably an abbreviation of St. Asaph, the C6th saint. Situated off A548 between Mostyn and Prestatyn. Double-aisled C16th church. White Lion Inn was boyhood home of actor and playwright Emlyn Williams, who wrote *The Corn Is Green.*

LLANBADRIG, Anglesey (Church of Patrick)
From A5025 take turn on unmarked road at point between Cemaes Bay and Amlwch. Reputed to be one of several places from which St. Patrick could have sailed to Ireland. Splendid view of coastline, but Wylfa Nuclear Power Station stands out incongruously. Church at end of farm road, in spectacular position. Dates from C14th. Very exposed, according to one account, in the past the verocity of the wind "prevented the performance of divine service".

LLANBEDR, Gwynedd
3 miles S of Harlech on A496. At church is stone with Bronze Age design indicating religious activity on site of village before Christian times. Was also the location of an RAF

base for many years, but on this site you will now find a holiday village; craft shops, adventure playground, nature trails, etc.

LLANBEDR DC, Denbighshire
On 494 2 miles from Ruthin on Mold Road. Victorian church contains monument by underrated Welsh sculptor John Gibson. C19th writer Leigh Hunt wrote over-sentimental poem praising area while staying at Llanbedr Hall.

LLANBEDROG, Llŷn
On A49 between Pwllheli and Abersoch. Sheltered from winds by sheer cliff. Popular resort with restored church approached by lych gate hidden by trees in Summer.

LLANBERIS, Gwynedd (Church of Peris) (Pop. 3,500)
Small town in shadow of Snowdon on A4086 between Capel Curig and Caernarfon. The most visited part of Snowdonia. Lies on SW shore of Llyn Padarn and is close to Llyn Peris to E. Snowdon mountain railway has operated here since 1896. Dolbadarn Castle built early C13th. Owain Glyndŵr is said to have imprisoned Lord Grey of Ruthin here. Was major slate quarrying area: quarrying museum.

LLANBERIS LAKE RAILWAY, Gwynedd
See Llanberis. Quarry railway opened 1840 to transport slates to Porthmadog harbour. Discontinued in 1961 and it now carries tourists the 2 miles around Llyn Padarn. Return journey takes 45 minutes.

LLANDYRNOG, Denbighshire
Church dedicated to St. Dyrnog has C19th interior. At nearby Llangwyfan there was once a well-known chest hospital which mainly treated TB cases.

LLANDDWYN ISLAND, Anglesey (Ynys Llanddwyn)
Promontory 1 mile long at S of Newborough Warren. This was the retreat of St. Dwynwen, patron saint of lovers. The ruined church dates from C16th. Lighthouse built in 1873. Previously a tower guided ships. A suitably romantic spot.

LLANGEFNI, Anglesey (Pop. 4,320)
En route to Holyhead turn R off A5 at Llangristiolus and drive for 11/2 miles. County town of Anglesey with parish church dedicated to St. Cyngor. John Wesley was scathing about town when he visited in 1748. Prestigious art gallery, Oriel Ynys Mon, well worth a visit. 1 mile from town.

LLANDEGAI, Gwynedd
Take A5 from Bangor to Bethesda. 2 miles S. Picturesque village built by Lord Penrhyn at castle gate. Restored church at end of yew tree avenue with interesting tombs and effigies.

LLANDDONA, Anglesey

In eastern part of island. Take turn off A5025 at Pentraeth. Village famed in Welsh history and folklore for its witches whose malevolent practices are reputed to have caused much distress.

LLANEILIAN CHURCH, Anglesey

From Amlwch take B coast road for 21/2 miles through Amlwch Port. C6th church where St. Eilian founded his cell and well. Much visited by pilgrims in earlier centuries. Has rood screen and medieval loft.

LLANDDEUSANT, Anglesey (Two Saints)

Take A5025 from A5 at Valley and turn R at Llanfachraeth. Llinon Mill, a windmill, recently restored and open to visitors during season. Flour still ground there.

LLANDUDNO, Conwy (Church of St. Tudno) (Pop. 19,530)

On 546 situated on outcrop of land connecting Great Orme's Head with the rest of Creuddyn peninsula. Victorian resort with impressive hotels. Cable cars and trams take visitors to summit. Orme ancient copper mines open to public. Dry ski slope, North Wales Theatre situated here and resort has good record in providing good family entertainment of many kinds over the years. Film *The Card*, with Alec Guiness, made on location in the resort in the Fifties. Unique in having two beach shorelines back-to-back. West Shore has monument to *Alice in Wonderland,* whose writer Lewis Carroll (Charles Dodgson) spent summer vacations here, in the building now the Gogarth Hotel. When he was in the resort in 1864 *Mathew Arnold* observed that it was "…alive with the Saxon invaders from Liverpool". According to *Arnold Bennett* in his novel *The Card* (1911) Llandudno was "… more stylish than either Rhyl or Blackpool and not dearer".

LLANDUDNO JUNCTION, Conwy

On A55 between Colwyn Bay and Conwy and so named due to its importance in terms of rail connections, especially in the C19th when it was fashionable to holiday in Llandudno and travel by train.

LLANDULLAS, Conwy

Village between St. Asaph and Colwyn Bay now by-passed by A55. Main industry of area has been quarrying. Terrible railway catastrophe occurred here in 1868 when a train hit trucks of petroleum. 28 burned to death. Evelyn Waugh, the novelist, taught at prep school here as young man in 1925 and recorded jaundiced impressions of the Welsh.

LLANFAIRFECHAN, Conwy (Pop. 3,700)

Village between Conwy and Bangor by-passed by A55. A hillside track (known as 'the Roman road') will take the energetic overland to the Conwy Valley. Lavan Sands (Traeth Lavan) stretch from Llanfairfechan almost to Anglesey coast, and down to Bangor. Tide comes in very quickly.

LLANFAES, Anglesey
On B6109 N of Beaumaris but nearer the mouth of the Straits. Llewelyn the Great granted Franciscans a site for a Friary here. Nothing remains today however.

LLANFAIRTALHAIARN
Church of St. Mary founded by Talhaiarn C6th, bard. Good location for exploration of Elwy Valley and situated on 548 between Llanrwst and Abergele. C19th poet Talhaiarn born at Harp Inn.

LLANFAIRPWLLGWYNGYLLGOGERYCHWYRNDROBWLLLANTYSILIO-GOGOGOCH, Anglesey (Llanfair PG) (Pop. 2,800)
Longest place name in the world. Translated this means — St. Mary's Church in a hollow by the white hazel near the rapid whirlpool and St. Tysilio's church by the Red Cave. Name board on railway station much photographed. Nearby is Anglesey column built 1816 to commemorate the first Marquis of Anglesey for his action at Waterloo. 91ft high with 15 steps. See Plas Newydd.

LLANFAIRYNGHORNWY, Anglesey
Village in NW corner of Anglesey in parish which includes The Skerries (See separate entry). Parish church underwent major C19th restoration. Area associated with the remarkable family of Bone Setters who in the C18th became the early pioneers of orthopaedic surgery.

LLANFAETHLU, Anglesey
On A5025 in SW of island. Quiet village 1 mile from sea. St. Maethlu's Church Victorian. Village within close proximity of Porth Trefadog, an unspoiled bay in rural surroundings where an ancient castle once stood.

LLANFAIR, Denbighshire (Church of St. Mary's)
2 miles S of Ruthin on A525. Usually referred to as Llanfair DC to differentiate it from the other places of same name in Wales. Beautiful church with Vale-of-Clwyd style double nave.

LLAN FFESTINIOG, Gwynedd
A village on the A470 between Blaenau Ffestiniog and Trawsfynydd. Situated at the head of the Ffestiniog valley it makes a good starting point for walks. Slate quarrying remains. When he came to the area in 1774 *Lord George Lyttleton* extolled its qualities: "With the woman one loves, with the friend of one's heart, and a good study of books one might pass an age in this vale and think it a day".

LLANFYLLIN, Powys (Myllin's Church) (Pop. 1,503)
On A490 12 miles N of Welshpool. Good base for exploration of borderland. Situated on river Cain, tributary of Vyrnwy. Many Georgian red-brick buildings inc church and Town Hall of 1791. Close to Llanwddyn Valley.

LLANGELYNIN, Gwynedd
61/2 m N of Tywyn on A493. Ancient church founded by Celynin. It was believed that a water stoup was kept miraculously filled.

LLANGERNYW, Conwy
Between the vales of Conwy and Clwyd on A548 Llanrwst road.Church founded by St. Digain in C5th whose father is said to have been British king Cystenyn Gernev. Roman remains discovered here. Cultural importance: birthplace of two remarkable C19th scholars, Henry Jones and Robert Roberts.

LLANGWYFAN, Denbighshire
East of Denbigh. The large house Fron Yw — now a retirement home — was the residence of the Madock family. They lived 600 years in the Vale of Clwyd. They descend from a Governor of Dyserth Castle in the reign of Henry II. John Madocks of Bodfari (1601-1662) was the first to use the family name. John Madock in the late C18th was a successful London lawyer. His son William Alexander Madocks was a MP for Boston, Lincolnshire. He created the 'ideal' community of Tremadog and after building the Cob or causeway between Porthmadog and Penrhyndendraeth, started the slate boom of the mid C19th.

LLANIDAN OLD CHURCH, Anglesey
From Brynsiencyn on A4080, and beyond the present church, turn L at lodge down narrow lane. Church lies close to Menai Straits. Following Dissolution of Monasteries it became

Llangollen Bridge

Waterfall, Llanrhaeadyr-ym-Mochnant

parish church, but most of it demolished in 1844. Ruin, but still one of the most romantic spots in Anglesey.

LLANGOLLEN, Denbighshire (Pop. 4,650)

Town in Dee Valley on A5 between Chirk and Corwen. In C7th church of St. Collen was built here. After period as Abbot of Glastonbury he retired to this lovely valley beside the Dee. Dee bridge c1345 and extended since. World famous as venue of International Musical Eisteddfod held early July. ECTARC centre reflects aspects of European folk culture. Canals and horse-drawn excursions. Llangollen steam railway takes passengers on 5-mile journey to Berwyn. Plas Newydd, home of the Ladies of Llangollen, open Easter-September. See Dinas Bran. When the composer *Mendelssohn* visited the town in 1829 he heard a local harpist playing national airs, but this had a disgruntling affect on him and he described the music as 'dreadful, vulgar, out-of-tune trash" and complained that it gave him toothache. During his stay in 1872 *Francis Kilvert* also heard a harpist but his reaction was more favourable: "I would have come all the way to Llangollen on purpose to hear the Welsh harp".

LLANGYNHAFAL, Denbighshire

Church dedicated to Cynhafal, a C7th saint. Church lies up lane to E of village and interesting features include a hammer-beam roof with curved angels. Impressive pelican lectern. Next to church is Plas-yn-Llan, half-timbered house where Wordsworth once stayed with his undergraduate friend Robert Jones.

LLANGWYFAN BEACH, Anglesey
Can be reached on Rhosneigr-Holyhead by-pass. Bay of Prince Llewelyn's chief residence. Very sandy. Small offshore rocky island on which C7th church of St. Gwyfan lies.

LLANRHAEADR DC, Denbighshire
Attractive village by-passed by A525 4 miles from Denbigh on Ruthin Road. Fine C15th double-aisled church is well worth a visit. Praised by John Betjeman because of its fine Jesse Window, one of most interesting in Britain. Glass buried in chest for preservation during ravages of Cromwellian soldiers during Civil War. Well in wood behind church.

LLANRHAEADR-ym-MOCHNANT, Powys
(Llan — church; rhaeadr — waterfall; moch — pig; nant — brook or valley)
On A590 N of Tanat Valley. Bishop William Morgan was appointed to living of parish in 1578 and undertook mammoth task of translation from original sources into Welsh of the two Testaments of the Bible: took him nine years. Village used for location of 1995 feature film *The Englishman Who Went Up A Hill and Came Down A Mountain*.

LLANRHYCHWYN CHURCH, Conwy
From Llanrwst take B5106 for 2 miles. Roof timbers 800 years old and oldest font in Britain. It is thought that Prince Llewelyn worshipped here.

LLANRWST, Conwy (Pop. 2,856)
Can be reached on B5156 road from Betws-y-Coed. On east bank of Conwy, which is spanned by famous three-arch bridge (1636) ascribed to Inigo Jones. Nearby cafe and gift shop Tu-Hwnt-i'r-Bont is very old. Church has many important features. 1 miles from town is Tudor mansion Gwydir Castle, former seat of the Wynn family. In private ownership but access granted to public on request. On the bridge *A. G. Bradley* observed that it had the capacity to shake when struck forcibly on the parapet above its centre: "... there is generally a loafer about who, for the price of a pint of beer, is only too anxious and willing to convince the sceptical upon this point". (1897).

LLANSANNAN, Conwy
Church dedicated to Senau, Irish saint and bishop of C6th. Situated on A544 between Bylchau and Llanfair TH. Situated in Aled Valley. In main street is Goscombe John's memorial stone commemorating local luminaries, including William Rees (Gwilym Hiraethog) C19th editor and writer who took his name from Hiraethog region in which Llansannan is situated. During First World War prisoner-of-war camp located in area. Two German naval officers made unsuccessful endeavour to get away but were caught at Llandudno.

LLANUWCHLLYN, Gwynedd (Church above the Lake)
Village off A494 near head of Bala Lake. Birthplace of O. M. Edwards, an important educationalist and writer whose work resulted in the establishment of the Urdd Gobaith Cymru, a cultural youth movement. Commemorated by statue.

LLANYNYS, Denbighshire
From A525 Denbigh-Ruthin road turn at Pentre Llanrhaeadr down minor road. Village is on flat land at heart of Vale of Clwyd and rivers Clwyd and Clywedog flow here. Church next door to Cerrigllwydion Arms, contains rare mural of St. Christopher, the patron saint of travellers. C14th hexagonal headstone.

LLANYSTUMDWY, Gwynedd
Rivers Dwyfor and Dwyfach meet here. Dwy was old word for goddess of a river. Ystum means a bending river. On A496 2 miles W of Criccieth. Boyhood home of David Lloyd George. Museum perpetuates his life and work. Open Easter-October. Highgate Cottage, early home, next door and also open to public.He is buried on banks of River Dwyfor very close to village.

LLECHWEDD SLATE CAVERNS, Blaenau Ffestiniog
On A470 between Betws-y-Coed and Porthmadog. Explore underground world of slate quarrying by tramway. Shops, smithy, etc. Open throughout season.

LLIW FALLS, Conwy
Turn off B5106 Conwy-Llanrwst road at halfway point. Miniature Swallow Falls. River Lliw is split by enormous boulders as water descends. Moorland surroundings. Visitors should seek permission to visit the fall from nearby farmhouse.

LOGGERHEADS, Flintshire
Country park 4 miles from Mold on A494 Ruthin road. Woodland walks along the River Alyn. Nature trails, countryside centre and restaurant.

LLYN IDWAL (Idwal Lake) GR6457
In the Glyder group of mountains, 1,223 ft. up and covering 28 acres. Like many Snowdonian lakes, shrouded in myth and legend. One of most interesting sites in Britain for study of glaciation formations, as Charles Darwin discovered in last century. Also extremely popular with rock climbers. Writer Showell Styles wrote ballad about it. One of few places where Snowdon Lily grows.

M

MACHYNLLETH, Powys (Pop. 2,200)
Place name means 'plains of Cynllaith'. Situated in green valley of Dyfi. C16th building Owain Glyndwr Institute where the leader held his first parliament in 1404. Prominent clock tower in main street built 1872. Celtica Centre opened in 1995 exploring in technically adept ways elements of Celtic myth and history. 3 miles away, up the valley of river Dulas, is Centre for Alternative Technology, which will appeal to all concerned about energy creation and the quality of our environment. In 1485 Henry Tudor and his army were joined at Machynlleth by Rhys ap Thomas, the only powerful man in Wales to declare for him openly. The army marched eastwards to Bosworth Field,where

Richard III was killed. Henry becomes Henry VII, the first Tudor monarch (1453-1509).

MAENAN, Conwy
Take A470 S of Bodnant. Nothing remains of old abbey. Present building 1848. Abbey moved from Aberconwy at mouth of Conwy at time of Edward I. Romans active here during their occupation.

MAENTWROG, Gwynedd (Rock of Twrog)
Twrog was C15th saint. Village between Ffestiniog and Harlech. Church has ancient stone with legendary associations with giant. It has also been suggested that it marks burial place of Pryderi who figures in *The Mabinogion.* Writer Thomas Love Peacock lived briefly in area. Snowdonia Study centre Plas Tan-y-Bwlch here.

MAEN-Y-BARDD, Conwy
Turn off B106 to Rowen between Conwy and Llanrwst. Burial chamber with massive capstone 1800BC. Stands on rocky slope from which panoramic view of valley may be obtained. Close to old Roman Road along Tal-y-Fan mountain.

MAES GARMON, Flintshire
1 mile W of Mold. Site of C5th battle. Picts were defeated by Christians and much blood was shed.

MAES ACHWYNFAN, Flintshire ("Stone of Lamentation")
Situated at Whitford, off A55 N of Holywell. A noted Christian cross which reveals Viking influence.

MALLTRAETH, Anglesey
On A4080. Mall means corrupt and traeth beach. In low flat valley beside stretch of tidal water parallel to Menai Straits. Malltraeth cob built early C19th. At low tide large areas of sand revealed.

MALLWYD, Gwynedd
Small village situated in S Gwynedd on junction of A470 and A458. Strongly associated with tales of Red Bandits in C15th, and a local pub is called 'The Brigand's Inn'. Borrow visited Mallwydd and wrote of these thieves in *Wild Wales.*

MAWDDACH, Gwynedd
As you travel along A496 between Barmouth and Dolgellau the Mawddach estuary lies on your right. Has its source in the Aran Mawddwy upland region. Poet Gerard Manley Hopkins wrote poem about Penmaenpool and John Ruskin extolled natural beauty of area.

MENAI BRIDGE, Anglesey (Porthaethwy)
Menai derived from Roman Mona. This small town situated 5 miles from Telford's suspension bridge on the A545 Beaumaris road. Venue of well-known annual horse fair.

Yachting and watersports.

MIGNEINT, Conwy (Area of Bog)
A sheepfarming area of remote moorland lying at over 1,000 ft. with magnificent views of the Arenigs. Situated between the A5 at Pentrefoelas and the Llan Ffestiniog area. The B4406 runs through the region. Marvellous drive on unfenced road through rolling uplands. Beware of sheep!

MOLD, Flintshire (Yr Wyddgrug) (Pop. 9,250)
On A494 W of Queensferry and 11 miles NW of Wrexham.Old county town of Flintshire. Situated on River Alyn. C15th parish church worth a visit. Birthplace of C19th novelist Daniel Owen. Theatr Clwyd, prestigious arts complex on outskirts of town close to County Hall.

MOEL FAMMAU, Denbighshire
The highest hill in the Clwydian range (1,820 ft.). On summit are ruins of commemorative tower built to celebrate 50th anniversary of reign of George III. Easy path to summit. Turn off A494 Mold-Ruthin road at Llanbedr DC. See Clwydian Range.

MOELFRE, Anglesey (Bare Hill)
Take A5025 N between Menai Bridge and Amlwch. Creek sheltered by headland overlooking small island. Popular resort with harbour and lifeboat station. A bloody battle took place in the area in the 11th century.

MOEL HEBOG, Gwynedd (Hill of the Hawk)
Craggy mountain to S of Beddgelert. 2,566 ft. Site of cave which was reputed to be hideout of Owain Glyndŵr. Remote, densely forested, hillside.

Menai Bridge, Anglesey

MOEL SIABOD, Conwy
Fairly easy ascent from Capel Curig by crossing Pont Cyfyng at lower end of village. Those who go up will be rewarded with fine views.

MORWYNION LAKE GR 6500
Take B4391 W across Migneint. Remote upland lake associated with drowned maidens in *The Mabinogion*. In earlier times nearby stones marked Beddau Gwyr Ardudwy, 'the graves of the men of Ardudwy'. 5 Acres.

MYMBYR LAKES, Conwy GR 7057
Twin Capel Curig lakes popular with canoists. Plas-y-Brenin situated close to lower lake. Used as mountain warfare centre during last war. Popular with landscape painters. 5 miles W of Snowdon.

MYNYDD HIRAETHOG, Conwy
This upland moorland region extends from the Conwy to the Clwyd valley and the A543 traverses the region, connecting the A5 with Denbigh. The mynydd (mountain) is also called 'Denbigh Moors'. Sheepfarming main source of employment for farmers. Area rich in culture, folklore and legends. Gwylfa Hiraethog is a ruined shooting box at centre of moors (near Sportmans Arms) and very prominent landmark.

N

NANNAU, Gwynedd
At head of estuary of river Mawddach, this historic house built 1100 and was seat of Vaughan family. One of Vaughans attempted to murder Owain Glyndŵr.

NANNERCH, Flintshire
Name denotes a combination of nant, stream and erch, coloured. 10 miles NW of Mold off Denbigh road. Interesting old water mill and craft centre. Rising Sun Inn occupies site where there has been a hostelry for 500 years.

NANT COL, Gwynedd
Situated off the A496 Barmouth-Harlech road. Turn off at Llanbedr and proceed up minor side road. On R side you will come to cottage-like building which is, in fact, a chapel. It was here that C19th painter Curnor Vosper painted a local woman in shawl in which, it is claimed, the devil's face may be seen.

NANT FFRANCON, Gwynedd (Vale of the Beavers)
This spectacular area of Snowdonia is bordered by the Carnedds to the S. Runs from Bethesda to Llyn Ogwen. Exposed and treeless; popular with wild life observers.

NANTGLYN, Denbighshire
S of Denbigh on B4501, a village near the head of the Ystrad valley. St. James's Church has yew tree 1,000 years old in which slate pulpit is built. Welsh scholars associated with

area: poet Twm o'r Nant and William Own Pugh. Also David Samwell, physician and poet, who sailed with Captain Cook on final ill-fated expedition.

NANT GWYNANT, Gwynedd
Can be approached on the A498 Beddgelert to Pen-y-Gwryd road. Runs past the flank of Snowdon. Glaslyn flows down the tree-lined valley. Llyn Gwynant here. Excellent picnic place.

NANT GWTHEYRN, Gwynedd (Vortigern's Valley)
From Nefyn B4417 5½ miles E to Llithfaen. Turn L until you reach car park. Walk 3/4 mile down zig-zag path to village. Not for vehicles or the unfit. Vortigen had castle here destroyed by "fire from heaven" — or so legend has it! A very neat village of ex-fishermen's cottages many of which form a complex of residences for Welsh-learners; in this lovely spot one of world's oldest languages is being given new lease of life.

NANT FALLS, Gwynedd
From Caernarfon take A487 Beddgelert road. After Waunfawr look for signpost. Easy access and sometimes referred to as 'the artists paradise'. Also has appeal for garden lovers because of display of azaleas and hydrangeas. Close to ruins of Nant Mill.

NEFYN, Gwynedd
On A497 which crosses Llŷn from Pwllheli. Church here though to be dedicated to Nefyn, C5th saint. Edward I celebrated conquest of Gwynedd here. See Morfa Nefyn.

NEWBOROUGH WARREN, Anglesey
From minor road from Newborough take minor well-signposted road. Extensive area of sand dunes on designated nature reserve. Toll payment for cars. Access to St. Dwynwen's island (see separate entry). One of the best beaches in North Wales.

O

OFFA'S DYKE (Clawdd Offa)
C7th mound built by King Offa of Mercia to keep Welsh out. Footpath runs for total of 173 miles, from Sedbury Cliffs, near Chepstow, to Prestatyn. Visitor centres at Rhaeadr and Prestatyn.

OGWEN COTTAGE, Gwynedd
On A5 between Capel Curig and Bethesda. Cottage on roadside on W side of Llyn Ogwen. Reputedly designed by Telford, it is now an outdoor pursuit centre owned by Birmingham LEA. Frequented by the great names of British mountaineering.

OGWEN LAKE, Gwynedd GR 6560
Can be reached on A5 from point close to Bethesda. Shallow lake covering 78 acres. As in C19th, it is still in ownership of Penrhyn estate. Old drovers' showing station was con-

verted into wartime pill box and used by Home Guard. Good angling lake.

OVERTON
S of Wrexham on A5069. Georgian architecture. St. Mary's church, restored 1870, surrounded by yews. Overton bridge spans Dee in village.

P

PADARN LAKE, Gwynedd (Llyn Padarn) GR 5761
Padarn was ancient saint whose origins have been lost in time. The most dominant lakeside feature is Dolbadarn castle. Its twin lake is the Peris; originally one lake but over period of thousands of years silting has caused a separation and formation of one extensive stretch of water over 280 acres. Scene of tragedies over the years, most recent being accident involving Wessex helicopter in 1993, which crashed into lake killing 3 cadets.

PANTASAPH, Flintshire (Hollow of Asaph)
2 miles W of Holywell. Catholic community founded by the Earl and Countess of Denbigh in 1852. Church contains fine woodcarvings. Hilly wooded pilgrimage path takes one through the stages of the Cross to Calvary on the summit.

PANT GLAS (from the Welsh 'blue valley')
A hamlet about half-way between Porthmadog and Caernarfon on the A487. Where Bryn Terfel (Jones) grew up and where his parents farm. His magnificent baritone voice is heard in opera houses around the world.

PARYS MOUNTAIN, Anglesey (Mynydd Parys)
2 miles S of Amlwch on B5025. At 500 ft. it looks like a volcanic crater with red ochre, yellow and purple rock. Mined by Romans for copper and opened up again in C18th. Visitors of that period described result of toxic fumes emitted. See Kinmell Hall.

PENMAENMAWR, Conwy
By-passed by A55 between Conwy and Llanfairfechan. Quarrying has taken place here since Stone Age. Axe heads and other ancient tools discovered. Popular resort in late C19th visited by Gladstone and Elgar. Sheltered by mountains. Black sheep of the Bronte family, Branwell, wrote poem about the area.

PENMACHNO, Conwy (Head of the Machno)
3 miles SE of Betws-y-Coed on B4406. Was productive slate quarrying village until decline of industry. Bishop William Morgan, who translated both Testaments of Bible into Welsh, born 1545 at Tŷ Mawr in nearby Wybrnant Valley. Woollen mill with shop. William Morgan is commemorated on monument at St. Asaph Cathedral.
PENMAENPOOL, Gwynedd. On A493 N of Fairbourne. On loop of river Mawddach spanned by wooden toll bridge. Poet Gerald Manley Hopkins stayed at inn nearby and wrote poetic comments in visitors' book.

PENMON PRIORY, Anglesey
From Beaumaris take B5109 N and turn R at crossroads. Continue for 1/2 mile and turn at T junction and continue to priory car park. Close to Menai Straits and founded by Cynlas in C16th but was destroyed by Danes in C12th. Rebuilding took place. Dove côte is C16th and deep park, at rear of building, C18th.

PENMYNYDD, Anglesey
Village between Llangefni and Llanfairpwll. Nearby farmhouse of that name home of the Tudors. Henry VII's great grandfather lived here. Present building dates from 1576 and is in private ownership. Tudor coat of arms at local church.

PENNANT MELANGELL, Powys
Take B4391 from Bala and turn R up minor road at Llangynog. Proceed for 21/2 miles up this upper part of Tanat valley until you arrive at this hamlet. Has charming Norman church with 2 recumbent effigies. Loft of the screen has mutilated carvings showing scenes from legend of St. Malangell, patron saint of hares. Valley ends in rounded cwm and facing you in the distance is Blaen-y-Cwm waterfall.

PENNANT VALLEY, Gwynedd
Take side road off A487 half-way between Morfa and Glyn Dwyfach at Dolbenmaen. Head of this Snowdonia valley closed by semi-circle of peaks. Eifion Wynn wrote: "Oh God, why didn't thou make Cwm Pennant so beautiful and the life of the shepherd so short?"

PENRHYN CASTLE, Gwynedd
Opulent granite building built 1827-37, although estate dates back to time of Llewelyn the Great. Home of slate quarry owning magnate George Douglas Pennant. In 1859 he entertained Queen Victoria here. In 1949 estate passed to niece of 4th Baron Pennant and in 1951 his niece granted permission for National Trust to administer it. See Llandegai.

PENSARN HARBOUR, Gwynedd
2 miles S of Harlech on A496. At mouth of river Nantcol; built 1700 for coastal trade of coal and limestone. Wreck 100 yards N believed to be that of *Unity of Barmouth* built around 1830.

PENTREFOELAS, Conwy (Village of the green hill)
Small estate village on A5 between Cerrig-y-Drudion and Betws-y-Coed. In mid C19th there were over 50 trades being pursued here. Close to Denbigh Moors.

PERIS LAKE, Gwynedd (Llyn Peris) Llanberis GR5959
Peris was ancient Saint who founded church at Nant Peris. Rocks at lower end can be interpreted as silhouette of woman's head gazing westwards. In 1974 a pump storage scheme was constructed here, the largest of its kind in Europe.

PISTYLL RHAEADR, Powys

4 miles from Llanrheadr-ym-Mochnant. At the end of the village take minor road; well signposted. The fall descends 240 ft. and is highest in Wales. Much admired by George Borrow. Visited by Dr. Johnson in late C18th. One of 7 wonders of Wales.

PISTYLL Y CAIN, Gwynedd

Can be reached on A470 road between Gwynfynydd and Ganllwyd. The noise of this waterfall can be heard down the valley. 2 mile walk to falls through gorge by Mawddach. Best viewed from wooden bridge before Mawddach Falls. Formerly source of water power for gold mines.

PLAS MAWR, Conwy (Big House)

Large Elizabethan manor house in centre of Conwy; widely acknowledged as best preserved town house in Wales. Built by Robert Wynne. Said to be haunted by three-year-old child and its mother. For many years has been the main exhibition area of the Royal Cambrian Art Society. Open to public.

PLAS NEWYDD, Anglesey (New Palace)

Seat of Marquess of Anglesey. Present Marquess lives there although house is maintained by National Trust. Very fine house with sweeping lawns and magnificent views. Artist Rex Whistler painted murals in the house. Open to public.

PLAS TAN-Y-BWLCH, Gwynedd

Originally built as a mansion during the C19th this fine building is now the Snowdonia Study Centre and residential courses on a variety of topics relating to the area are held throughout the year. A station on the Ffestiniog narrow gauge railway line is also called Tan-y-Bwlch and is close by. From Maentwrog you will see the building dominating the scene between the trees on the opposite side of the valley.

POINT LYNAS, Anglesey

W of Amlwch on headland. Promontory offers good view of coastline. Present lighthouse built here 1835.

PORTDINORWIC, Gwynedd (Felinheli)

On A487 between Bangor and Caernarfon. Important in last century as a quay. Rees Jones, of Barmouth, established ship building business here in 1824 the object being the transportation of slate from the quarries. (The harbour belonged to Dinorwic quarry).

PORTMEIRION, Gwynedd

Situated between Penrhyndeadraeth and Porthmadog on the A487. Well signposted. Unique Italianate village conceived by Clogh Williams-Ellis; he described it as his "home for distressed buildings". TV series *The Prisoner* was filmed here and visitors have included Noel Coward, Edward VII and Bernard Shaw. Exotic trees. A top Welsh tourist attraction.

Portmeirion, Penrhyndeudraeth

PORTHDINLLAEN, Gwynedd
8 miles NW of Pwhelli on A497. Sandy sheltered beach almost 2 miles long. Good bathing, car park and cafes. Golf.

PORTHMADOG, Gwynedd (Harbour of Madog) (Pop. 3,000)
On A487 E of Criccieth. The Cob, long embankment carrying road and Ffestiniog Railway across mouth of Glaslyn, built by W. A. Madocks in early C19th as part of reclamation of 7000 acres of Traeth Mawr. Slates in massive numbers were brought on the Ffestiniog Railway, down from Blaenau Ffestiniog through Penrhyndendraeth ('the headland with two beaches') across the cob to Porthmadog. Schooner sailing boats were

Porthmadog, Gwynedd

built locally and exported the slates to distant ports including Buenos Aires, Boston and Hamburg. When young man Lloyd George practised as a solicitor here; he grew up at nearby Llanystumdwy. Look for his surname on a window in the High Street.

PORTH YSGAGAN, Gwynedd
From Nefyn SW along B4417 to Tudweiliog. Was C17th-18th centre of herring fishing trade. Many disputes among fishermen, and an admiral arbitrated in disputes and sometimes courts were held out at sea.

POWYS CASTLE, Powys
Can be reached on A483 1 miles S of Welshpool. First castle built by Owain ap Gruffydd against threat of border barons. The present castle is set in gardens designed by Capability Brown. State rooms open to public. Douglas Fir in grounds reputed to be tallest in Britain.

PRECIPICE WALK, Gwynedd
W of Llanelltyd on A496. 3 mile circular walk overlooking glacial valley of river Mawddach. Laid out as nature trail with signposts and picnic tables. Area of great beauty.

PRESTATYN, Denbighshire
On A548 coast road between Connah's Quay and Rhyl. Much evidence of Roman settlement here, including bath house. From later period there is C12th motte and bailey defence. Mainly residential resort much favoured by elderly. Northern end of Offa's Dyke Footpath.

PUFFIN ISLAND, or Priestholm, Anglesey (Ynys Seiriol)
Just off tip of Anglesey and N of Beaumaris. Named after C6th St. Seiriol. Ruins of C12th church. Occupied by holy men during Middle Ages. In C19th a semaphore station established here.

PWLLHELI, Gwynedd (Pool of salt water) (Pop. 4,250)
Good centre for touring the Llŷn. Created a borough by Black Prince. Grew as resort in Victorian period but has also figured prominently in maritime history, but ship building industry moved to Porthmadog in 1820's. Fine long beach with adjacent road. Magnificent new yatching marina.

QUEENSFERRY, Flintshire
On A494 W of Ewlowe. Ferry from which it takes name long since replaced by two road bridges over Dee at N entrance to Wales near Chester. Has extensive leisure centre, ice rink and sports arena.

R

RED WHARF BAY, Anglesey

On A5025 between Menai Bridge and Benllech. The haunt of curlews and oyster catchers. Yachting. Popular with painters. Atmospheric old pub at sea level.

RHAIADR DDU GANLLWYD, Gwynedd (The Dark Waterfall)
Situated off A470. Its dark waters slide vertically into even deeper depths. Smaller falls below. Pleasant walk along banks of River Gamlan.

RHINOGS, Gwynedd
Can be approached from Llanbedr on A496 Harlech-Barmouth road. Two mountains, Rhinog Fawr (2,362 ft.) to the N and Rhinog Fach, which is not of same height. Wild, remote area, which includes Llyn Cwm Bychan. Paved pack-horse trail rises from valley of Cwm Bychan and is commonly referred to as 'the Roman steps'.

RHIW, Gwynedd
On Llanbedrog-Aberdaron road. Hilltop hamlet near tip of Llŷn. Sheltered by 1,000 ft. Mynydd Rhiw is C16th manor house, Plas-yn-Rhiw, with splendid grounds. Run by National Trust.

RHOSLLANERCHRUGOG, Wrexham (Moorland dotted with cairns)
One of conurbation communities which have evolved through coal mining around Wrexham. From Wrexham take A483 Ruabon road and turn at Ponciau. Has strong cultural tradition evolving from Nonconformity. Famous male voice choir. Meredith Edwards, star of many British cinema films, born here. In atmosphere it allies itself with certain South Wales communities and is unlike anywhere else in the North.

RHOS-ON-SEA, Conwy (Llandrillo-yn-Rhos)
Residential, suburban area between Colwyn Bay and Llandudno but joined with Colwyn Bay. Evolved in C19th. Focal point tiny C6th chapel of St. Trillo on foreshoe. Still used for worship.

RHOSTRYFAN, Gwynedd
As you travel along the A4085 take turn before Waunfawr. Good base for hill walking. Hills tend to have such biblical names as Carmel. At Rhosgadfan is the shell of a cottage which was childhood home of Welsh novelist Kate Roberts. It is preserved as a tribute to her.

RHUDDLAN, Denbighshire (Pop. 3,500)
On A525 Rhyl-St. Asaph road. Norman castle built by Edward I. Original bridge over Clwyd 1595. Statute of Rhuddlan 1283; see commemorative plaque on Old Parliament House, High Street. Community important in maritime history of area. Visited, and written about, by great American novelist Nathaniel Hawthorne in 1853.

RHYD-DDU, Gwynedd
Village close to Llyn Cwellyn and 31/2 miles N of Beddgelert on the A4085. Popular as walking centre; an ascent to Snowdon begins in village.

St. Peter's Square, Ruthin

RHYL, Denbighshire (Pop.. 23,000)
Evolved from C19th fishing village to major Welsh resort thanks to the railway. Clwyd enters sea at Foryd harbour. World's first hovercraft passenger service ran from Rhyl to the Wirral and first submarine sank off Rhyl. Has new Pavilion Theatre.

RIVALS, Gwynedd
Hills to N of Nevin rising to 1,849 ft. much quarried on seaward side. On E peak is Tre'r Ceiri, ancient British camp with ruined walls and circular cells.

ROSSETT, Wrexham
Village on A433 N of Wrexham and within 1 mile of Cheshire border. Black and white mill C14th with surviving wheel and machinery last used 1961. Headquarters of field sports organisation WAGBI.

ROWEN, Conwy
Off the B5106 S of Conwy. Roman road passed closed to village on route to Caerhun. Splendid views.

RUTHIN, Denbighshire (Pop. 4,200)
Name probably corruption of rhudd, red and din, town; red soil in the area. In heart of Vale of Clwyd 71/2 miles from Denbigh. Several attractive old buildings around St. Peter's Square and a fine church with ornate carvings on ceilings. Original castle here probably Norman. In 1400 Owain Glyndŵr and his men attacked Ruthin. On banks of river Clwyd. Stone near bank on square is one on which King Arthur is said to have executed Huail, a love rival. Craft Centre well worth a visit. The American novelist

Nathaniel Hawthorne visited Ruthin in 1853 and thought it "an exceedingly old looking place" and observed "…witch-like women very unlike anything feminine in America".

S

SARN BADRIG, Gwynedd
Popular name for St. Patrick's Causeway, long rocky reef 14 miles out to sea off Harlech. Traditionally it is said to have been a kingdom. A maiden left the top off a holy well, water erupted out and whole region became flooded.

SARN HELEN, Gwynedd
S of Trawsfynydd and fairly close to Ffestiniog. Remains one of the great Roman roads through Wales.

SEALAND, Flintshire
On the A548 6 miles from Chester, on right bank of the Dee. Flat reclaimed land. Garden City and RAF airfield. St. Bartholemew's church C19th.

SEGONTIUM, Gwynedd
From Caernarfon take A487 Beddgelert road from 1/2 mile. This Roman fort lies at the termination of the Roman road from Chester. Low walls outline what were once buildings and street. Open to public.

SEVERN RIVER (Afon Hafren)
River flows through Welsh border country, and meets the Wye at Chepstow. Historically has played significant role as boundary and was invasion route for Welsh raiders. Many disputes settled on its banks.

SHELL ISLAND, Gwynedd (Mochras)
Turn off Harlech-Barmouth road at Llanbedr: well signposted. Not an island but a peninsula, the name Mochras meaning many shells. 170 species of wild flowers have been identified here. Sandy beaches, dunes, camping and boating. Also shops, snack bar and restaurant.

SHOTTON, Flintshire
On the A548 road W of Queensferry. Main historical focus is on steel production, the Summers family having chosen it as a suitable industrial site in late C19th. When this closed down in 1975 many men were out of work.

SKERRIES, Anglesey
Jagged rocks two miles off Carmel Head known as 'the island of the seals', (Ynysoedd y Moelrhoniaid) and within parish of Llanfairynghonwy on NW part of Anglesey. Site of important lighthouse, guiding shipping along treacherous stretch of coastline; established 1716.

SMALLEST HOUSE IN WALES, Conwy

Situated on the N part of Conwy quay. Curious building with total frontage of 72 inches. Adjoins town walls. Built in C18th and the last inhabitant was a 6ft 3in tall fisherman who left in 1900. Open to public.

SNOWDON, Gwynedd (Y Wyddfa Fawr)

3,560 ft. high, making it the highest mountain in England and Wales. Highest in a series of five peaks, linked by sharp ridges. Easiest but longest walking route begins at Llanberis, but less energetic may ascend on the Snowdon Mountain Railway. (see separate entry). Restaurant and gift shop at summit, and cairn.

SNOWDON MOUNTAIN RAILWAY

Operates between Easter and late October each year, the return journey taking 21/2 hours, which includes 1/2 hour on the summit. This narrow-gauge rack-and-pinion line is the only one in Britain and was established in 1896. The Snowdon Summit station is just below the cairn. The views en route are magnificent.

ST. ASAPH, Denbighshire (Pop. 3,000) (Llanelwy)

Situated on A525 at halfway point between Rhyl and Denbigh and by-passed by A55. St. Kentigern founded settlement here in C6th and the Cathedral is thought to have been built on this site. Asaph came later. Rivers Clwyd and Elwy meet close to the city, the second smallest in Wales; the smallest is St. David's.

ST. GEORGE, Conwy (Llan Sain Sior)

21/2 miles from Abergele off A55 in St. Asaph direction. Small village so named because of legendary conflict between St. George and the dragon. Very old yew trees in churchyard. Healing well for sick animals in parkland nearby.

ST. HYWYN'S CHURCH, Gwynedd (Eglwys St. Hywyn's)

At water's edge in Aberdaron. Ancient C12th church well-known for its provision of sanctuary in less tolerant times. S aisle added in C16th. The church yard wall is washed by the sea at high tide. This church was the last living place of the poet R. S. Thomas. He retired from here to live in Rhiw, nearby, and later moved to Anglesey.

ST. MARY'S CHURCH, Llanaber, Gwynedd

On A496 road 11/2 miles N of Barmouth. Stands very close to edge of Cardigan Bay and dates back to C13th. Contains several features of architectural interest and an old alms chest. In early C18th French ships would unload supplies of brandy which was then stored in hollow tombs in the graveyard.

ST. MARY'S WELL, Denbigshire (Ffynnon Fair)

3 miles W of St. Asaph in field on banks of Elwy. Holy well and ruins of holy chapel similar in design to the shrine at Holywell, but much smaller. Well suppressed in 16th

and worship ceased here in C17th. Used for clandestine marriages for a time. Less than a mile from Cefn Caves. On private land and visitors need to apply for permission to view it.

ST. WINIFREDE'S WELL, Flintshire (Ffynnon Winifrede)
This shrine gives its name to Holywell, where it is situated. Has been pilgrimage site for 1300 years. Spring traditionally associated with the severing of Winifrede's head by unwanted suitor, but it was miraculously replaced by her uncle. Well and chapel among finest Gothic building in Wales. See Holywell.

SWALLOW FALLS, Conwy
On A5 2 miles W of Betws-y-Coed. River Llugwy joins with Conwy beyond Capel Curig and adds impetus to this torrent.It falls into a 60 ft. chasm between jagged rocks. Folklore has it that the tyrranical Sir John Wynne of Gwydr was doomed to remain under the falls to be purged following his death. Admission charge.

SYCHNANT PASS, Conwy
This road rising to 550 ft. links Conwy and Penmaenmawr and can be approached along the A55. Sharp bends. Pull in at a high point and you will be rewarded with a fine vista of the coastline.

T

TALACRE, Flintshire
Village on A548 between Prestatyn and Flint. Sand dunes and, on the shore, a lighthouse.

TALARGOCH LEADMINE, Denbighshire
Situated at Dyserth 3 1/2 miles E of Rhyl at foot of promontory on which once stood Dyserth Castle. Was worked from Roman times up to last century. Coins discovered during excavations dating to Roman period.

TANAT VALLEY
Turn off A43 after Oswestry and take B4396 signposted to Llanrhaeadr-ym-Mochnant. Railway was built up valley in order to transport slate from Llangynog. The eventual objective was to reach the sea at Porthmadog, but this came to nothing due to difficulties of terrain of the Berwyns.

TOMEN Y MUR, Gwynedd
Roman auxiliary fort amphitheatre. From Maentwrog go SE on A470 for 2 miles pass junction with A470 and take first turn on L. Proceed under low railway bridge and carry on for one mile, leaving car beyond cattle grid. Amphitheatre and adjoining earthworks are open but fort itself is on private land, and permission should be sought by visitors at nearby Tyddyn Du farm.

TYWYN, Gwynedd
Town on the A493 between Barmouth and Aberdyfi. Church of St. Cadfan at N part of town named after founder in C4th, who also established the monastery on Bardsey Island. The St. Cadfan Stone has an inscription which is the earliest known example of written Welsh. Town best known as terminus of the Talyllyn Railway. (See separate entry).

TRAWSFYNYDD, Gwynedd
South of Ffestiniog on A470. Small village close to large man-made lake. Trawsfynydd Nuclear Power Station opened 1957 and open to public. Birthplace of Hedd Wynn, the Welsh poet, killed in First World War and posthumously given chair at Birkenhead Eisteddfod. Film based on his life won acclaim.

TREARDDUR BAY, Anglesey
Follow A5 to Valley, turn left and cross to Holy Island by Four Mile Bridge. Wide inlet facing SW, numerous small bays and good bathing. No promenade. Church dedicated to St. Bridget.

TRE'R CEIRI, Gwynedd
On eastern peak of the Rivals on Llŷn, this is the largest hillfort in North Wales. In outline it is still possible to see the prehistoric town which stood here.

TREFNANT, Denbighshire
Name is a compound of Tref, homestead,and nant, stream. Situated on the A525 2 miles S of St. Asaph. A Victorian village which evolved during 'railway boom'. A typical church of the period. Site of toy factory during First World War.

TREFRIW, Conwy
Village on W bank of Conwy 5 miles N of Betws-y-Coed on the B5106. Focal point for visitors is Roman spa, which became very popular in Victorian times. The sulphur iron waters are said to be among most beneficial in the world. Admission charge. Busy woollen mill.

TRELAWNYD, Flintshire (Newmarket)
On A5151 between Rhuddlan and Holywell. It has a very large prehistoric cairn on Cop Hill (to the N) and has a fine male voice choir, which has competed in many competitions. The Gop Bone Cave excavated 1886 and 1908 and artefacts discovered. Was thought to have been inhabited in 4th millennium BC. Animal bones found and hence the bone reference.

TREMADOG, Gwynedd (Town of Madog)
Village situated 1 mile N of Porthmadog on A487. Built by W. A. Maddocks in early C19th and largely unspoiled. Remains a notable example of community planning of its period. Lawrence of Arabia was born here in 1888 and a plaque com-

memorates this outside his birthplace. Shelley and his wife stayed at Madock's house, Tan-yr-Allt in 1813, where he said an attempt to murder him and his 'wife' was made.

TREMEIRCHION, Denbighshire
Village SE of St. Asaph. Turn off A55 to 5429. Has delightful C13th church; a tablet commemorates Hester Thrale, close friend of Dr. Samuel Johnson. She lived at the nearby mansion Bryn Bella. 1 mile from village is St. Beuno's Jesuit College, established in 1840's. Great English poet Gerard manley Hopkins underwent his training for the Jesuit priesthood here between 1874 and 1877 and wrote of the area in some of his work. The poem *Pied Beauty* was written here, and describes the view down to the Vale of Clwyd.

TREFOR, Gwynedd
On A499 between Nefyn and Clynnog Fawr. Just below the Rivals, this is a quarrying village at end of a minor road. Owes its existence to houses built here for quarry workers. Trefor stone was used for monumental purposes and curling stones.

TRYFAN, Gwynedd
A noble mountain at 3,010 ft. and extremely popular with climbers. In shape it resembles a pyramid and there are two stones on the summit known as Adam and Eve.

TUDNO'S CRADLE, Conwy
Above Happy Valley at Llandudno is an eminence called Pen-y-Dinas. Close to this is the rocking stone often referred to as Tudno's Cradle. See Happy Valley.

TWYN Y WYLFA (The Hill of Weeping)
Legend relates how the inhabitants of fertile plain between Puffin Island and Great Orme climbed up this hill away from a flood which covered their homes.

TY COED UCHA, Conwy
This farm is situated at Penmachno and is preserved by National Trust. Here you can step into the Welsh rural past of the C19th and house is furnished accordingly. Fields carefully conserved and containing rare varieties of meadow plants. Has been open to public since April 1994.

TY CRWN, Gwynedd (The Round House)
Built in 1882, this lock-up can be found on the quay at Barmouth and was built by the Harbour Trust for jailing of drunken sailors and other ner-do-wells. They were detained here before appearing before the local magistrate

TY NEWYDD BURIAL CHAMBER, Anglesey
Can be reached on A4080 Holyhead-Rhosneigr road. Bronze Age artefacts have been found inside chamber. Capstone damaged but repaired some years ago.

U

UGLY HOUSE, Conwy (Ty Hyll)
On the A5 between Betws-y-Coed and Capel Curig. So called because of its rough appearance. Was said to have been built very quickly in order to beat the deadline for a freehold on what was common land. Once an overnight stop for Irish drovers en route from Holyhead to markets in England. Open to public.

V

VALLE CRUCIS, Denbighshire
Take A542 at Llandegla and proceed down 'Horseshoe Pass' in direction of Llangollen. Ruined Cistercian Abbey founded 1201 by Madog ap Gruffydd, a Prince of Powys. Abbey dissolved 1535, but despite ravages of time it is well preserved ruin. Visited by Borrow in 1854. Thought to be the burial place of Welsh bard Iolo Goch.

VALLEY, Anglesey
On A5 Bangor-Holyhead road in N of the island. Given its name by Telford when he was constructing road in last century later to become A5. Was home of Iron Age man but is today best known as a military air base, built in 1941. Among other things base is used for training purposes. Nearby lake source of precious artefacts from the Celtic period (including a gold torc) now in the Museum of Wales, Cardiff.

VARDRE, Conwy
Take A5115 N of Llandudno Junction. Hill rises immediately behind Deganwy and on top are remains of Deganwy castle. Was frequently mentioned in Welsh history as a seat of Maelgwn Gwynedd in C6th and he is said to have met Gildas here on one occasion. The slight ruins visible are those of medieval castle built in 1211 by an Earl of Chester. Henry III besieged here by the Welsh, but in 1263 Deganwy finally destroyed by Llewelyn the Last.

VYRNWY LAKE (Llyn Efyrnwy)
On B4393. Turn off A490 near Llanfyllin. Provides domestic water supply to Liverpool and was constructed in 1886-1890. 4 miles in length and 1/2 mile wide. The dam is 390 yards long and 144 ft. high. Lakes surface area 1,121 acres and its storage capacity 12,131 million gallons. Visitors centre and RSPB observation post.

W

WAENFAWR, Gwynedd
7 miles S of Caernarfon on A4085. First major village on old Roman road. Centre for walking in the foothills.

WATERLOO BRIDGE, Conwy
On A5 between Betws-y-Coed and Pentrefoelas. Graceful iron bridge over the Conwy built by Telford to commemorate the famous battle of 1815. There is an inscription on the parapet.

WELSH MOUNTAIN ZOO, Conwy
Situated at Colwyn Bay — from the town follow signpost via King's Road. 37 acre wooded estate overlooking coast and Conwy Valley. Home of a number of wild animals. Monkey house, aviaries, lion pen, alligators, etc. Flying displays of birds of prey. Restaurant and gift shop. Excellent for a family outing.

WREXHAM (Pop. 120,000) A new county borough which was created as a result of the reorganisation of county boundaries in 1995. Previously the area which now comprises the county was in the county of Clwyd. The civic offices are located at Wrexham.

WREXHAM, Wrexham (Pop. 42,500)
Name probably compound of rex and ham, kings hamlet or village. Largest town in North Wales, its nearness to English border makes it Anglicised. Transformed from rural town to industrial centre during C19th industrial period. Became centre for coal and iron. St. Giles' Church is burial place of Elihu Yale, benefactor of Yale University. Steeple one of 7 wonders of Wales. Its football team, in Division Two, has following across North Wales. 'Capital of North Wales'. The population of the County Borough is 123,000. It has 16,131 who speak Welsh. When *George Borrow* visited Wrexham in 1854 he was told that "the people are fond of good ale" and, appropriately, there is still a prominent brewery here today, and Wrexham Lager is famous throughout Europe.

Y

YNYS, Gwynedd (Island)
Turn off the A496 between Maentwrog and Harlech to this peaceful and beautiful stretch of the estuary looking out to Traeth Mawr and Portmeirion; within the area known as Morfa Harlech. Called Ynys because of island in estuary, which has a mariners' chapel. Many sea birds.

YSBYTY-IFAN, Conwy
Remote village reached from A5. Turn off on B4407 near Pentrefoelas, on road which eventually leads to Ffestiniog. In 1189 the Knights of St. John of Jerusalem established a hospice and sanctuary here, and this became well-known in Middle Ages. A cinema film version of Emlyn Williams' play "The Corn Is Green" was made on location here many years ago and starred Katherine Hepburn.

YSCEIFIOG, Flintshire

Turn off the A541 Denbigh-Mold road at Afonwen. An ancient settlement with a number of tumuli. In Middle Ages it was important resting place for travellers. Both the Fox Inn and the Rectory are C18th.

Z

ZOO, Welsh Mountain
See entry under W.

ALSO AVAILABLE FROM JOHN JONES PUBLISHING LTD

FEET IN CHAINS by Kate Roberts. Translated from the Welsh by John Idris Jones. "Her characters are motivated by the need to survive poverty with some dignity, independence and self-respect. She is skilful at her craft, welding her short chapters into a strong bridge to link the generations and decades she writes about." *Tribune* "I urge it strongly for its distillation of time and place and people ... triumphantly alive in their own small corner." *The Guardian* "A seminal work of Welsh-language fiction and one which has drawn praise from critics, not only in Wales but in England and America. It remains one of the finest novels which I have read by any writer." Dewi Roberts *Cambrensis* 1996 "It is a mark of the compelling power of this short novel and the vitality of its translation by John Idris Jones that it seems important we should know what Kate Roberts was really saying ... we admire the force of this narrative ..." Richard Jones *The New Welsh Review* Autumn 1996

ISBN 1 871083 80 X   Price £4.99

TEA IN THE HEATHER by Kate Roberts. Translated by Wyn Griffith. Eight stories set in Caernarfonshire in the early years of the twentieth century. They are clear, historically accurate accounts of the lives of smallholding hill farmers and quarrymen, holding their culture together in the face of deprivation. There is a central link in the presence of the girl Begw; the first story presents her at the age of about three; in the last one she is nine. Her friend Winni is a rebel, old before her time. These are moving, unforgettable stories.

ISBN 1 871083 85 0   Price £4.99